KT-572-890

FATHERED
BY
GOD

Other Books by John Eldredge

Walking with God

The Ransomed Heart

Captivating
(with Stasi Eldredge)

Epic

Waking the Dead

Wild at Heart

The Journey of Desire

The Sacred Romance
(with Brent Curtis)

FATHERED BY GOD

JOHN ELDREDGE

THOMAS NELSON
Since 1798

NASHVILLE   DALLAS   MEXICO CITY   RIO DE JANEIRO

© 2009 by John Eldredge

All rights reserved. No portion of this book may be reproduced, stored in a retrieval system, or transmitted in any form or by any means—electronic, mechanical, photocopy, recording, scanning, or other—except for brief quotations in critical reviews or articles, without the prior written permission of the publisher.

Published in Nashville, Tennessee, by Thomas Nelson. Thomas Nelson is a registered trademark of Thomas Nelson, Inc.

Published in association with Yates & Yates, LLP, Attorneys and Counselors, Orange, California.

Thomas Nelson, Inc., titles may be purchased in bulk for educational, business, fund-raising, or sales promotional use. For information, please e-mail SpecialMarkets@ThomasNelson.com.

Scripture quotations marked NIV are from the HOLY BIBLE: NEW INTERNATIONAL VERSION®. © 1973, 1978, 1984 by International Bible Society. Used by permission of Zondervan. All rights reserved.

Scripture quotations marked NASB are from the NEW AMERICAN STANDARD BIBLE®. © The Lockman Foundation 1960, 1962, 1963, 1968, 1971, 1972, 1973, 1975, 1977, 1995. Used by permission.

Scripture quotations marked MSG are from *The Message* by Eugene H. Peterson. © 1993, 1994, 1995, 1996, 2000. Used by permission of NavPress Publishing Group. All rights reserved.

Scripture quotations marked NKJV are from THE NEW KING JAMES VERSION. © 1982 by Thomas Nelson, Inc. Used by permission. All rights reserved.

Scripture quotations marked NLT are from the *Holy Bible*, New Living Translation. © 1996. Used by permission of Tyndale House Publishers, Inc., Wheaton, Illinois 60189. All rights reserved.

ISBN: 978-0-7852-0677-4 (hardcover)
ISBN: 978-0-7852-8868-8 (IE)

Library of Congress Cataloging-in-Publication Data

Eldredge, John.
    The way of the wild heart : a map for the masculine journey / John Eldredge.
        p. cm.
    ISBN: 978-1-4002-8027-8
        1. Christian men—Religious life. 2. Masculinity—Religious aspects—Christianity. I. Title.
BV4528.2.E447 2001
248.8'42—dc22   2006013989

Printed in the United States of America

11 12 13 14 RRD 16 15

TO POP

CONTENTS

How gladly would I treat you like sons . . .

—JEREMIAH 3:19 NIV

INTRODUCTION

ONE OF THE MOST HAUNTING EXPERIENCES I HAVE EVER had as a man took place on an early summer day in Alaska. My family and I were sea kayaking with humpback whales in the Icy Strait, and we stopped on the shore of Chichagof Island for lunch. Our guide asked us if we wanted to go for a hike into the interior of the island, to a clearing where grizzlies were known to feed. We were all over that invitation. After a twenty minute walk through a spruce forest, we came into what appeared to be a broad, open meadow about four hundred yards across. Being midday, and hot, there were no bears to be seen. "They're sleeping now, through the afternoon. They'll be back tonight," he said. "C'mere—I want to show you something."

The meadow was actually more of a bog, a low-lying jungle of brushy groundcover about two feet high, barely supported underneath by another foot of soaked moss and peat. A very difficult place to walk. Our guide led us to a trail of what seemed to be massive footprints, with a stride of about two feet between them, pressed down into the bog and making a path through it. "It's a marked trail," he said. A path created by the footprints of the bears. "This one is probably centuries old. For as long as the bears have been on this island, they've taken this path. The cubs follow their elders, putting their feet exactly where the older bears walk. That's how they learn to cross this place."

I began to walk in the marked trail, stepping into the firm, deep-worn places where bears had walked for centuries. I'm not sure how to describe the experience, but for some reason the word *holy* comes to mind. An ancient and fearful path through a wild and untamed place. I was following a proven way, laid down by those much stronger and far more prepared for this place than me. And though I knew I did not belong there, I was haunted by it, could have followed that path for a long, long time. It awakened some deep, ancient yearning in me.

This is a book about what it looks like to become a man, and —far more to our need—*how* to become a man. This material was previously released in a book entitled *The Way of the Wild Heart* but we felt that many men (and women!) missed that message and so we have re-presented it here. There is no more hazardous undertaking, this business of "becoming a man," full of dangers, counterfeits, and disasters. It is the Great Trial of every man's life, played out over time, and every male young and old finds himself in this journey. Though there are few who find their way through. Our perilous journey has been made all the more difficult because we live in a time with very little direction. A time with very few fathers to show us the way.

As men, we desperately need something like that marked trail on Chichagof Island. Not more rules, not another list of principles, not formulas. A sure path, marked by men for centuries before us. I believe we can find it.

What you are holding in your hands is a map. It chronicles the stages of the masculine journey from boyhood to old age. This is not a book of clinical psychology, nor a manual of child development. For one, I am unqualified to write that sort of book. Further, I find them unreadable. Ponderous. Boring. What do you recall of your psychology textbook from high school or college? But I do love maps. Most men do. The pleasure of a map is that it gives you the lay of the land, and yet you still have to make choices about how you will cover the terrain before you. A map is a guide, not a formula. It offers freedom.

It does not tell you how fast to walk, though when you see the contour lines growing very close together, you know you are approaching steep terrain and will want to mend your stride. It does not tell you why the mountain is there, or how old the forest is. It tells you how to get where you are going.

A companion workbook is available to help you, and you'll *experience* a whole lot more of the journey if you do the workbook too. The best approach would be to read this first, *then* go back through it with the workbook. Maybe get a few guys to go through it together. The workbook is now available as a free download at www.ransomedheart.com/fatheredbygod. Share it with your group; copy it for your friends! (The workbook will not be available in stores.)

I've often wondered at the long lists found many places in the Bible that recount a roster of men as "the son of so-and-so, who was the son of so-and-so." You'll find many of these rosters in the Scriptures, and elsewhere in ancient literature. Perhaps these accounts reveal something we hadn't noticed before—a father-view of the world held by those who wrote them, shared by those who would read them. Perhaps they saw in the father-son legacy the most significant of all legacies, that to know a man's father was in great part to know the man. And then, if you step back further to have a look, you'll see that the God of the Bible is portrayed as a great Father—not primarily as mother, not merely as Creator—but as Father.

It opens a new horizon for us.

You see, the world in which we live has lost something vital, something core to understanding life and a man's place in it. For the time in which we live is, as the social prophet Alexander Mitcherlie had it, a time without a father. I mean this in two ways. First, that most men and most boys have no real father able to guide them through the jungles of the masculine journey, and they are—most of us are—unfinished and unfathered men. Or boys. Or boys in men's bodies. But there is a deeper meaning to the phrase "a time without a father." Our way of looking at the world has changed. We no longer live, either as a society or even as the church, with a father-view of the world, the view centered in the presence of a loving and strong father deeply engaged in our lives, to whom we can turn at any time for the guidance, comfort, and provision we need.

And that is actually an occasion for hope. Because the life you've known as a man is *not* all there is. There is another way. A path laid down for centuries by men who have gone before us. A marked trail. And there *is* a Father ready to show us that path and help us follow it.

I The Masculine Journey

Stand at the crossroads and look;
ask for the ancient paths,
ask where the good way is, and walk in it,
and you will find rest for your souls.
—Jeremiah 6:16 niv

All I was trying to do was fix the sprinklers.

A fairly straightforward plumbing job. The guy who came to drain our system and blow it out for the winter told me last fall that there was a crack in "the main valve," and I'd better replace the thing before I turned the water back on come next summer. For the past several days it had been hot—midnineties, unusually hot for Colorado in May—and I knew I'd better get the water going or my yard would soon go the way of the Gobi Desert. Honestly, I looked forward to the project. Really. I enjoy tackling outside chores for the most part, enjoy the feeling of having triumphed over some small adversity, restoring wellness to my domain. Traces of Adam, I suppose—rule and subdue, be fruitful, all that.

I disengaged the large brass valve from the system on the side of the house, set off to the plumbing store to get a new one. "I need one of these," I said to the guy behind the counter. "It's called a reducing valve," he replied, with a touch of condescension. Okay, so I didn't know that. I'm an amateur. Nevertheless, I'm ready to go. Valve in hand, I returned home to tackle the project. A new challenge loomed before me: soldering a piece of copper pipe to a copper fitting that carried the water from the house to the sprinklers, reduced in pressure by the valve now in my possession. It seemed simple enough. I even followed the instructions that came with the butane torch I bought. (Following instructions is usually something I do only once a project has become a NASCAR pileup, but this was new ground for me, the valve was expensive, and I didn't want to screw the whole thing up.) Sure enough, I couldn't do it, couldn't get the solder to melt into the joint as needed to prevent leaks.

Suddenly, I was angry.

Now, I used to get angry at the drop of a hat, sometimes violently angry as a teen, punching holes in the walls of my bedroom, kicking holes in doors. But the years have had their mellowing effect, and by the grace of God there has also been the sanctifying influence of the Spirit, and my anger surprised me. It felt . . . disproportionate to the issue at hand. I can't get a pipe soldered together. So? *I've never done this before. Cut yourself some slack.*

But reason was not exactly ruling the moment, and in anger I stormed into the house to try to find some help.

Like so many men in our culture—solitary men who have no father around to ask how to do this or that, no other men around at all, or too much pride to ask the men who are around—I turned to the Internet, found one of those sites that explains things like how to surmount household plumbing problems, watched a little animated video on how to solder copper pipe. It felt . . . weird. I'm trying to play the man and fix my own sprinklers but I can't and there's no man here to show me how and so I'm watching a cute little video for the mechanically challenged and feeling like about ten years old. A cartoon for a man who is really a boy. Armed with information and wobbling confidence, I go back out, give it another try. Another miss.

At the end of the first round I merely felt like an idiot. Now I feel like an idiot doomed to failure. And I'm seething. A counselor and author both by trade and by intuition, I am nearly always watching my inner life with some detached part of me. *Wow*, that part of me says. *Have a look at this. What are you so hacked off about?*

I'll tell you why I'm hacked. There are two reasons. First, I'm hacked because there's no one here to show me how to do this. Why do I always have to figure this stuff out on my own? I'm sure if some guy who knew what he was doing were here, he'd take one look at the project and tell me right away what I'm doing wrong, and—more important—how to do it right. Together, we'd tackle the problem in no time and my yard would be saved and something in my soul would feel better.

I'm also hacked because I can't do it myself, mad that I *need* help. Long ago I resolved to live without needing help, vowed to figure things out on my own. It's a terrible and common vow to orphaned men who found ourselves alone as boys and decided that there really is no one there, that men are especially unreliable, so do it yourself. I'm also ticked at God, because why does it have to be so hard? I know—this was a lot to get out of a failed attempt to fix my sprinklers, but it could have been a dozen other situations. Doing my taxes. Talking to my sixteen-year-old son about dating. Buying a car. Buying a house. Making a career move. Any trial where I am called upon to play the man but immediately feel that nagging sense of, *I don't know how this is going to go. I'm alone in this. It's up to me to figure it out.*

Now, I do know this—I know that I am not alone in feeling alone. Most of the guys I've ever met feel like this at some point.

My story does not end there. I had to drop the project and get to work, leaving torch, pipe, and tools on my porch out of the merciful rain—merciful because it might buy me twenty-four hours to get this figured out before the death of my yard. I had to make an important phone call at 4:00 p.m., so I set my watch alarm in order not to miss it. I made the call, but failed to notice that my alarm did not go off. That took place at 4:00 *a.m.* the next morning. (I hadn't noticed the little "a.m." next to the 4:00 when I set the thing.) I'd gone to bed with no resolution inwardly or otherwise, and bang—I was yanked out of a deep sleep at 4:00 a.m. to face it, and all my uncertainties. Wham—just as suddenly, I am hit with this thought: *Get it right.*

This is perhaps the defining vow or compelling force of my adult life: you are alone in this world and you'd better watch it 'cause there isn't any room for error, so Get It Right. The detached observer in me says, *Wow—this is huge. You just hit the mother lode. I mean, jeez—this has defined your entire life and you've never even put it into words. And now here it is and you know what this is tied to, don't you?* Lying there in the dark of my bedroom, Stasi sleeping soundly beside me, the broken sprinkler system lying in misery just outside the window by my head, I know what this is about.

It's about fatherlessness.

UNFINISHED MEN

A boy has a lot to learn in his journey to become a man, and he becomes a man only through the active intervention of his father and the fellowship of men. It cannot happen any other way. To become a man—and to know that he *has* become a man—a boy must have a guide, a father who will show him how to fix a bike and cast a fishing rod and call a girl and land the job and all the many things a boy will encounter in his journey to become a man. This we must understand: masculinity is *bestowed.* A boy learns who he is and what he's made of from a man (or a company of men). This can't be learned in any other place. It can't be learned from other boys, and it can't be learned from the world of women. "The traditional way of raising sons," notes Robert Bly, "which lasted for thousands and thousands of years, amounted to fathers and sons living in close—murderously close—proximity, while the father taught the son a trade: perhaps farming or carpentry or blacksmithing or tailoring."

When I was young, my father would take me fishing early on a Saturday morning. We'd spend hours together out there, on a lake or a river, trying to catch fish. But the fish were never really the issue. What I longed for was his presence, his attention, and his delight in me. I longed for him to teach me how, show me the way. This is where to drop that line. This is how you set the hook. If you can get a group of men talking about their fathers, you'll hear this core longing of a man's heart. "My father used to take me with him out in the field." "My father taught me how to play hockey, out in the street." "I learned to frame a house from my dad." Whatever the details might be, when a man speaks of the greatest gift his father gave him—if his father gave him anything at all worth remembering—it is always the passing on of masculinity.

This is essential, for life will test you, my brothers. Like a ship at sea, you *will* be tested, and the storms will reveal the weak places in you as a man. They already have. How else do you account for the anger you feel, the fear, the vulnerability to certain temptations? Why can't you marry the girl? Having married, why can't you handle her emotions? Why haven't you found your life's mission? Why do financial crises send you into a rage or depression? You know what I speak of. And so our basic approach to life comes down to this: we stay in what we can handle, and steer clear of everything else. We engage where we feel we can or we must—as at work—and we hold back where we feel sure to fail, as in the deep waters of relating to our wife or our children, and in our spirituality.

You see, what we have now is a world of uninitiated men. Partial men. Boys, mostly, walking around in men's bodies, with men's jobs and families, finances, and responsibilities. The passing on of masculinity was never completed, if it was begun at all. The boy was never taken through the process of masculine initiation. That's why most of us are Unfinished Men. And therefore unable to truly live *as* men in whatever life throws at us. And unable to pass on to our sons and daughters what *they* need to become whole and holy men and women themselves.

At the same time there are these boys and young men and men our own age around us who are all very much in need—desperate need—of someone to show them the way. What does it mean to be a man? *Am* I a man? What should I do in this or that situation? These boys are growing up into uncertain men because the core questions of their souls have gone unanswered, or answered badly. They grow into men who act, but their actions are not rooted in a genuine strength, wisdom, and kindness. There is no one there to show them the way.

Masculine initiation is a journey, a *process*, a quest really, a story that unfolds over time. It can be a very beautiful and powerful event to experience a blessing or a ritual, to hear words spoken to us in a ceremony of some sort. Those moments can be turning points in our lives. But they are only moments, and moments, as you well know, pass quickly and are swallowed in the river of time. We need more than a moment, an event. We need a process, a journey, an epic story of many experiences woven together, building upon one another in a progression. We need *initiation*. And, we need a Guide.

FATHERED ON THE SOUTH PLATTE

I moved to Colorado in August of 1991. There were many reasons involved in the move from Los Angeles—a job, a shot at grad school, an escape from the seemingly endless asphalt-smog-and-strip-mall suffocation of L.A.—but beneath them all was a stronger desire to get to the mountains and the wide-open spaces, get within reach of wildness. I couldn't have articulated it at the time, but my soul was yearning to take up the masculine journey that felt aborted in my early teens. And with that, I wanted to become a fly fisherman.

My dad and I fished together when I was young, and those are among my most treasured memories of him. He taught me first to fish with a worm on a bobber, and then to cast a spinning rod. He was not a fly fisherman, but I wanted to be. Around the age of twenty-five, I bought myself a rod and reel and began to try to teach myself—a pattern by which, unfortunately, I have learned most of what I've learned in my life. We often speak of a man who's done this successfully as a "self-made man." The appellation is usually spoken with a sense of admiration, but really it should be said in the same tones we might use of the dearly departed, or of a man who recently lost an arm—with sadness and regret. What the term really means is "an orphaned man who figured how to master some part of life on his own."

Back to fly-fishing. When we got to Colorado I learned of a section of the South Platte River known for its reputation as a fly fisherman's dream. "The Miracle Mile" was past its heyday, but still a place that the best fly fishermen headed to, and so I went. It's a beautiful stretch of river that flows through open ranchland between two reservoirs. The banks are low and spacious, with only the occasional willow—a forgiving place for a novice to learn to cast. I spent the good part of a morning in the river, seeing trout all around me but unable to catch even one. Every time I looked upriver there was this guy, rod bent double, laughing and whooping as he brought yet another giant rainbow to his net. At first I envied him. Then I began to hate him. Finally, I chose humility and simply wanted to watch him for a while, try to learn what he was doing.

I stood at a respectful distance up the bank, not wanting to appear as an encroacher on his beloved spot, and sat down to watch. He was aware of me, and after casting maybe two or three times and hooking yet another fish, he turned and said, "C'mon down." I forget his name, but he told me he was a fly-fishing guide by profession, and on his days off this was where he most liked to fish. He asked me how I was doing and I said, "Not good."

"Lemme see your rig." I handed him my rod. "Oh . . . well, first off, your leader isn't long enough." Before I could apologize for being a fishing idiot, he had taken out a pair of clippers and nipped my leader off completely. He then tied on a new leader with such speed and grace I was speechless. "What flies you been usin'?" "These," I said sheepishly, knowing already they were the wrong flies only because I figured everything I was doing was wrong.

Graciously he made no comment on my flies, only said, "Here— this time of year you want to use these," pulling a few small midges off his vest and handing them to me. He tied one on my tippet, and then began to show me how to fish his treasured spot. "C'mon over here, right next to me." If a fly fisherman is right-handed, the instructor typically stands close on his left so as not to take the for-ward cast in the ear or the back of his head. "Now—most folks use one strike indicator when they're fishing the fly below the surface [I felt good that at least I knew that—had read it in a book]. But that won't help you much. You've got to know you're getting a dead drift." Success in fly-fishing rests upon many nuances, but chief among them is your ability to present your fly naturally to the fish, which means that it drifts down with the current in the same fash-ion as the real food they see every day—without any tugging or pulling motion contrary to the speed and direction of the current. "The secret is to use two, even three. Like this."

After about ten minutes of coaching, he stepped out of the water to watch me—just as a father who's taught his son to hit a baseball steps back to watch, let the boy take a few swings all by himself. I hooked a trout and landed it. He came back into the water to show me how to release it. "I usually kiss mine on the forehead. Superstition." He laid one on the brow of the large rainbow and released it into the cold water. "Have fun," he said, and without looking back he went downriver about to the spot where I'd been fishing earlier and began to catch fish there, one after another. I caught fish too. And while that made me happy, there was a deeper satisfaction in my soul as I stood in the river, fishing well. Some primal need had just been touched and touched good. As I drove home I knew the gift had been from God, that he had fathered me through this man.

INITIATION

We aren't meant to figure life out on our own. God wants to father us. The truth is, he *has* been fathering us for a long time—we just haven't had the eyes to see it. He wants to father us much more intimately, but we have to be in a posture to receive it. What that involves is a new way of seeing, a fundamental reorientation of how we look at life, and our situation in it. First, we allow that we are unfinished men, partial men, mostly boy inside, and we need *initiation*. In many, many ways. Second, we turn from our independence and all the ways we either charge at life or shrink from it; this may be one of the most basic and the most crucial ways a man repents. I say "repent" because our approach to life is based on the conviction that God, for the most part, doesn't show up much. I understand where the conviction came from, battle it constantly myself, but still—it's faithless, is it not? We must be willing to take an enormous risk, and open our hearts to the possibility that God *is* initiating us as men—maybe even in the very things in which we thought he'd abandoned us. We open ourselves up to being fathered.

I'll admit, it doesn't come easily. A sort of fundamental mistrust is something we learn through the course of our days, built on that core mistrust in God we inherited from Adam. Making the switch will feel awkward. As Gerald May says, the more we've become accustomed to seeking life apart from God, the more "abnormal and stressful" it seems "to look for God directly." *Especially* as a Father, fathering us. But it is worth it. *It is worth it.* Worth allowing ourselves to be fathered, accepting that this new way of living will take some getting used to, and taking the posture that we'll do whatever it takes to get used to it.

What I am suggesting is that we reframe the way we look at our lives as men. And the way we look at our relationships with God. I also want to help you to reframe the way you relate to other men, and especially you fathers who are wondering how to raise boys. The reframing begins when we see that a man's life is a process of initiation into true masculinity. It is a series of stages we soak in and progress through. And as for God, I believe that what he is *primarily* up to at any point in a boy's or a man's life is initiating him. So much of what we misinterpret as hassles or trials or screw-ups on our part are in fact God fathering us, taking us through something in order to strengthen us, or heal us, or dismantle some unholy thing in us. In other words, initiate us—a distinctly masculine venture.

THE STAGES

If I were to sketch out for you the masculine journey in broad strokes, I believe this is how it unfolds, or better, how it was *meant* to unfold: Boyhood to Cowboy to Warrior to Lover to King to Sage. All in the course of about eighty years or so, give or take a decade or two.

Now, let me be quick to add that one cannot pin an exact age to each stage. They overlap, and there are aspects of each stage in every other. Watch a boy for an afternoon (a very good idea, if it's been some time since you were a boy), and you'll see the warrior, the cowboy, the king. Yet he is a boy, and it is *as* a boy he must live during those years. Great damage is done if we ask a boy to become a king too soon, as is the case when a father abandons his family, walking out the door with the parting words, "You're the man of the house now." A cruel thing to do, and an even more cruel thing to say, for the boy has not yet become a man, not yet learned the lessons of boyhood and then young manhood. He has not yet been a warrior, nor a lover, and he is in no way ready to become a king.

When we ask this of him, it is a wound equal to a curse, for in a moment he is robbed of his boyhood, and asked to leap over stages of masculine maturity no man can leap over. No, there is a path that must be taken. There is a Way. Not a formula. A Way. Each stage has its lessons to be learned, and each stage can be wounded, cut short, leaving the growing man with an undeveloped soul. Then we wonder why he folds suddenly when he is forty-five, like a tree we find toppled in the yard after a night of strong winds. We go over to have a look and find that its roots hadn't sunk down deep into the earth, or perhaps that it was rotten on the inside, weakened by disease or drought. Such are the insides of Unfinished Men.

To begin with, there is boyhood, a time of wonder and exploration. A time of tree forts and comic books, pollywogs and Popsicles. Snakes and snails and puppy dog tails, as the old nursery rhyme has it. Above all else, it is the time of being the beloved son, the apple of your father's eye. A time of affirmation. For though I maintain my premise laid out in *Wild at Heart*—that every man shares the same core Question, and that Question runs something like "Do I have what it takes?"—I believe that Question is far more urgent to the cowboy stage and after. Before and beneath that Question and a man's search for validation lies a deeper need—to know that he is prized, delighted in, that he is the beloved son. Our need for a father's love.

The cowboy stage comes next, around the period of adolescence (thirteen seems to be the year of transition), and it runs into the late teens to early twenties. It is the time of learning the lessons of the field, a time of great adventures and testing, and also a time for hard work. The young man learns to hunt or throw a curveball or break a horse. He gets his first car and with it an open horizon. He takes off into the woods alone, or with a few buddies, travels to Europe, becomes a ranger or a smoke jumper. A time of daring and danger, a time of learning that he does, indeed, have what it takes.

Sometime in his late teens there emerges the young warrior, and this phase lasts well into his thirties. Again, the stages overlap, and there is some aspect of them in every phase of a man's life. Whether six or sixty, a man will always be a warrior, for he bears the image of a warrior God (see Exod. 15:3). But there is also a time in a man's life when one of the stages is prominent. The warrior gets a cause and, hopefully, a king. He heads off to law school or the mission field. He encounters evil face-to-face, and learns to defeat it. The young warrior learns the rigors of discipline—especially that inner discipline and resolution of spirit you see in Jesus, who "set his face like flint" (Isa. 50:7 NIV) and could not be deterred from his mission. He might join the marines, or he might become a math teacher in the inner city, battling for the hearts of young people. That he gets a mission is crucial, and that he learns to battle the kingdom of darkness is even more crucial. Passivity and masculinity are mutually exclusive, fundamentally at odds with one another. To be a man he must learn to live with courage, take action, go into battle.

This is typically the time when he also becomes a lover, though it would be best for him and for her if he lived as a warrior for some time first. As I also described in *Wild at Heart*, too many young men do not get their Question answered as a young cowboy, and as an uncertain warrior they have no mission to their lives. They end up taking all that to the woman, hoping in her to find validation and a reason for living (a desperately fruitless search, as many men now understand). A lover comes to *offer* his strength to a woman, not to get it from her. But the time of the lover is not foremost about the woman. It is the time when a young man discovers the Way of the Heart—that poetry and passion are far closer to the Truth than are mere reason and proposition. He awakens to beauty, to life. He discovers music and literature; like the young David, he becomes a romantic and it takes his spiritual life to a whole new level. Service *for* God is overshadowed by intimacy *with* God.

Then—and only then—is he ready to become a king, ready to rule a kingdom. The crisis of leadership in our churches, businesses, and governments is largely due to this one dilemma: men have been given power, but they are unprepared to handle it. The time of ruling is a tremendous test of character, for the king will be sorely tested to use his influence in humility, for the benefit of others. What we call the midlife crisis is often a man coming into a little money and influence, and using it to go back and recover what he missed as the beloved son (he buys himself toys) or the cowboy (he goes off on adventures). He is an undeveloped, uninitiated man.

A true king comes into authority and knows that the privilege is *not* so he can now arrange for his comfort. He might be made president of a company or commander over a division; he might become a senior pastor or a high school basketball coach. This is the time of ruling over a kingdom. Hopefully, he draws around him a company of young warriors, for he is now a father to younger men.

Finally, we have the sage, the gray-haired father with a wealth of knowledge and experience, whose mission now is to counsel others. His kingdom may shrink—the kids have left the house, so he might move into something smaller. He steps down from his role as president, and his income may shift to savings and investments made while he was king. But his *influence* ought to increase. This is not the time to pack off to Phoenix or Leisure World—the kingdom needs him now as an elder at the gates. He might in fact be an elder in his church, or he might serve on the board of education. His time is spent mentoring younger men, especially kings, as Merlin mentored Arthur, as Paul mentored Timothy. At a time in life when most men feel their time has passed, this could be the period of their greatest contribution.

Now, let me say again that these stages are all present to some degree at any period in a man's life, and they all come together to make a whole and holy man. The boy is very much a king of a little kingdom—his bedroom, the tree house, the fort he has built secretly in the basement or woods. And the man, though now a king in a far more serious manner, must never lose the wonder of the boy, that condition we call "young at heart." For by maturity we do not mean rigidity, calcification of the heart. As George MacDonald said, "The boy should enclose and keep, as his life, the child at the heart of him, and never let it go . . . the child is not meant to die, but to be for ever fresh-born." Jesus spoke to this when he said we must become like a child if we would live in his kingdom (Matt. 18:3).

Having said this, it does seem to me that each of the stages—archetypes, they might be called—does have a season when it comes into its own, when it seems to dominate and for good reason. So, I will speak of the stages in both respects.

IMAGERY OF THE STAGES

David might be the definitive biblical expression for the masculine journey. His life as a man is apparently worth giving special attention to, since God devotes sixty-some chapters of his book to David's life, whereas most of the other guys are lucky to get a paragraph or two. When we meet David he is in the cowboy stage, a teenager living out in the fields, watching over the family flocks. I thought to call this stage the Shepherd stage, but the word has been so badly hijacked by religious imagery it now conveys the opposite of the life it actually was. Our images of shepherds have been framed by Christmastime, through the charming little figurines found on coffee-table crèche displays or, closer to my point, the neighborhood kids in bathrobes, with towels on their heads, playing the role in the local pageant. They are cute. Actual shepherds are *rugged*.

On the eve of his passage from cowboy to warrior, David

stands in the camp of the army of Israel, before his king, who is trying to dissuade the teenager from single-handed combat against a notorious mercenary (Goliath). David says, "Your servant has been keeping his father's sheep. When a lion or a bear came and carried off a sheep from the flock, I went after it, struck it and rescued the sheep from its mouth. When it turned on me, I seized it by its hair, struck it and killed it" (1 Sam. 17:34–35 NIV). Those experiences came during his cowboy stage, and we see here how rugged and dangerous that stage is meant to be. We also see that he learned its lessons rather well. Was David ever the beloved son? It's difficult to tell. We have no record of his boyhood per se, though we do have two other pieces of information that might fill in to some degree. He was the youngest of eight boys, and that can be good and that can be bad. Typically, the youngest is the apple of his father's eye—as were Joseph, and Benjamin. But when you read the Psalms, there can be no doubt that David knew he was a beloved son of God; his poems are filled with the kind of heartfelt assurances of God's love and favor that only a beloved son can express.

As for the warrior, can there be any doubt that David sets the bar for this stage? "Saul has slain his thousands, and David his tens of thousands" proclaimed the women of Israel (1 Sam. 18:7 NIV). He was a lover, to be sure—though our thoughts probably jump at this point to the affair with Bathsheba. But it is from David we learn that the lover stage is *not* first about women at all—it is about the life of the heart, the life of beauty and passion and a deep romance with God, all of which can be seen in his poetry. And of course, David was, literally, a king.

You see the stages also in the life of Jesus. Surely, he is the beloved son, both of his parents and of God. The brief account we have of his childhood contains the story of when Jesus disappeared from the caravan his family was traveling with as they left the feast of the Passover in Jerusalem. What is remarkable is that it took Mary and Joseph two days to notice the boy was missing—demonstrating either gross parental neglect (a theory unsupported by the rest of what we know about the family) or remarkable security and assurance in the boy. And of course, much more to the point of our own journey here in this book, we have the pronouncement by God the Father over Jesus as he rises from the waters of the Jordan, "This is My beloved Son" (Matt. 3:17 NKJV). The confidence Jesus has in his Father's love, their bold and unquestioned intimacy, is the hallmark of his life, the explanation for everything else. This man knows his Father adores him.

I would place the cowboy years of Jesus' life in the carpenter's shop, hour upon hour at Joseph's side, learning woodcraft from his father and all the lessons lumber and hand tools have to teach a young man. A wonderful way for a teen to spend those years. Apparently he is comfortable in the wilderness as well, for he often goes there during his ministry years to be restored, to be with God his Father.

He enters the warrior phase as he enters his ministry, a three-year period marked by intense warfare, climaxing when he vanquishes the evil one, secures our ransom from the dungeons of darkness, wrestles the keys of hell and death from his enemy. Over the course of those years we also see a passionate lover wooing and winning the heart of his Bride. (And it might be good to remember that the Song of Songs was authored by the Spirit of God, who is without doubt the greatest lover of all time.) And of course, he is King, Lord now of heaven and earth, and a returning Warrior King who will bring final victory to his people and usher in the golden era of his realm. His earthly life was cut short, but even still we see the sage in the depth and insight of his masterful teaching. Of course, he is our Wonderful Counselor even now.

You'll Find the Stages Everywhere

Now that you have an outline for the Stages of the masculine journey, you will see them throughout all the great stories.

The Prince of Egypt, based on the life of Moses, is our first example. When the story begins he is a beloved son—spoiled, no doubt, and in great need of passage into the cowboy stage—but a beloved son nevertheless. His parents saw something special in the babe, and risked their lives to save his. Moses is adopted into Pharaoh's house, raised there in the life of privilege. He is hurled into the cowboy phase out in the wilderness, as a shepherd (which, as I said, was a rugged and demanding life, full of danger and adventure). Then, upon the call of God to free his people, he becomes a warrior and then the king and sage of the Israelites as they make their sojourn to the Promised Land.

Consider also J. R. R. Tolkien's trilogy, The Lord of the Rings. Each of the main characters is an image for a stage or several stages. The hobbits—especially Frodo—are a picture of the beloved son. Strider is the paramount cowboy (a "ranger," as they are called, a title you might easily substitute for "cowboy" wherever I talk about this stage). Then he becomes the great warrior Aragorn, who becomes king. Gandalf is their Sage. Looking closer, you can also see a boy's journey into manhood through the lives of the hobbits, whose journey-story it is. When we meet the hobbits they are living in the stage of the beloved son—curly hair, good-hearted, mischievous—their shire world a safe place they are free to explore. When they take to the road, they enter the cowboy stage. Yes, they have a mission, but they do not fully appreciate its gravity. At first it is a joy to be on the road, camping out, seeing new sights, experiencing life beyond a feather pillow. Aragorn takes them "into the wild," where they begin to be toughened, sleeping on the ground, enduring weather, danger, long treks. They go on to become warriors, learn to battle, go to war.

The stages also form the story line for the movie The Lion King. The opening scene announces the arrival of the lion cub Simba. He is the beloved son of the lion king Mufasa, and clearly the apple of his father's eye. But his youth is cut short by a sudden loss of innocence—as happens with so many boys—and he is hurled into the cowboy stage, taking to the road. However, he has no Aragorn to guide him, and his time in this stage is corrupted by staying in it too long, and living only for today. This happens to many fatherless young men, who live in adventure for adventure's sake, snowboarding, surfing, refusing to grow up. Simba enters the lover stage when Nala finds him in the forest, and they enjoy a sort of Edenlike idyll. But he is an aimless lover, as are so many young men who have not first passed through the warrior stage, and Nala grows impatient with him, as so many young women grow impatient with the young men they love but who show no signs of getting on with their lives.

Fortunately for Simba and for the realm, he is at this juncture found by a sage—the old baboon Rafiki—who takes him back to the father, and with that return come his true identity and call. He is restored to a father-centered world—the very restoration we also need. It is time for Simba to complete his journey into manhood, as warrior and king. He goes back to face his enemy, triumphs over the evil one, assumes the throne, and ushers in a new golden age for the kingdom.

TAKING UP THE QUEST

Thus our journey of masculine initiation. Now, we don't know much about stages of development in our instant culture. We have someone else make our coffee for us. We no longer have to wait to have our photos developed—not even an hour—for now we have digital cameras that deliver back to us the image, instantly. We don't have to wait to get in touch with someone—we can e-mail them, page them, call them on a cell phone, instant-message them this moment. We don't need to wait for our leather jackets or our jeans or caps to age to get that rugged look—they come that way now, prefaded, tattered. Character that can be bought and worn immediately.

But God is a God of *process*. If you want an oak tree, he has you start with an acorn. If you want a Bible, well, he delivers that over the course of more than a thousand years. If you want a man, you must begin with the boy. God ordained the stages of masculine development. They are woven into the fabric of our being, just as the laws of nature are woven into the fabric of the earth. In fact, those who lived closer to the earth respected and embraced the stages for centuries upon centuries. We might think of them as the ancient paths. Only recently have we lost touch with them. In exchange for triple-venti nonfat sugar-free vanilla lattes. The result of having abandoned masculine initiation is a world of unfinished, uninitiated men.

But it doesn't have to be this way. We needn't wander in a fog. We don't have to live alone, striving, sulking, uncertain, angry. We don't have to figure life out for ourselves. There is another way. Wherever we are in the journey, our initiation can begin in earnest. Far better for us—and for those who have to live with us, who look to us—to rediscover the stages and honor them, live within them, raise our sons through them. Which brings us back to our predicament: who is going to do this for us?

2   True Son of a True Father

I will be a Father to you,
and you will be my sons . . .
—2 Corinthians 6:18 niv

The time is the Middle Ages, 1184 anno Domini,
the year of our Lord. The time between the Second and Third
Crusades. A young man, a blacksmith called Balian, has lost both
his wife and son. And with them, because of their tragic deaths, he
has also lost his faith. He is certainly losing heart. As he hammers
away in his little smithy, a mysterious figure rides up on horseback,
apparently a lord of some sort, armed, asking for shoes for his
horses. The captain of a company, he studies the silent, angry
young man, watches him at work. He then announces to Balian
that he is his true father—Godfrey, Baron of Ibelin, a great warrior
returning to Jerusalem with a company of men. He invites Balian
to come with him.

At first the young man refuses. Why? Perhaps he has lost the capacity to hope. Perhaps the years of fatherlessness have caused him to mistrust this alleged father. You might answer for him, for his story is also ours in many ways. A fatherless man labors alone under the sorrows of his life. His true father comes to him, a vague and somewhat imposing figure, and calls him on a journey. The man hesitates, as we hesitate, unsure of the father and his intentions. How would you have responded, given the circumstances? Think about it. It might help you understand how you will respond to the offer God is extending to you.

After Godfrey rides away, Balian changes his mind, catches up with the men in the forest, hoping to find in Jerusalem—for he has heard it to be so—the forgiveness of his sins. A step in the right direction. Balian follows his father, if only to find forgiveness, as so many good men in the church believe in God, if only for forgiveness. But the father intends much more. Godfrey embraces Balian as his beloved son, heir to his domain (Rom. 8:17). He gives men in exchange for his life (Isa. 43:4). They take to the road together—for Balian, it is the time of the cowboy. His father trains him to be a warrior, and initiates him into the knighthood. He fathers Balian into the great mission of his life, to serve the true king of Jerusalem.

The kingdom of heaven is an insightful picture of the masculine journey, and we can be greatly helped by pictures like this one. As Norman Maclean wrote, "The nearest anyone can come to finding himself at any given age is to find a story that somehow tells him about himself." This is a good story to begin with. And there are many others to come.

FATHERLESS

You are the son of a kind, strong, and engaged Father, a Father wise enough to guide you in the Way, generous enough to provide for your journey, offering to walk with you every step.

This is perhaps *the* hardest thing for us to believe—really believe, down deep in our hearts, so that it changes us forever, changes the way we approach each day.

Of the thousands of conversations I've had with men over the years, in a counseling office or around a campfire, and of all the personal struggles that fill the pages of my own journals, I believe this is *the* core issue of our shared dilemma as men. We just don't believe it. Our core assumptions about the world boil down to this: we are on our own to make life work. We are not watched over. We are not cared for. Whatever our fathers might have provided, we are not much different now than Balian at the start of his story. When we are hit with a problem, we have to figure it out ourselves, or just take the hit. If anything good is going to come our way, we're the ones who are going to have to arrange for it. Many of us have called upon God as Father, but, frankly, he doesn't seem to have heard. We're not sure why. Maybe we didn't do it right. Maybe he's about more important matters. Whatever the reason, our experience of this world has framed our approach to life. We believe we are fatherless.

Just yesterday I was on the phone with a young friend about to enter his final year of grad school. We were chatting about all the pressures and demands that go with such a time in life—and a new marriage added to the equation—when I asked him a question designed to change the direction of the conversation, lift his eyes to the horizon. "Sam, what is bringing you joy these days?" A moment's pause. He then began to talk about a sea kayak he was saving up for, hoped to purchase come September. "But I feel like God is opposed to it." The comment struck me as odd. It felt . . . out of the blue. "Why?" I asked. "I don't know," he said. "I guess I find it hard to believe that he wants anything good for me." Ah, yes. This young man would not be alone in that feeling.

Sam began to wonder out loud about his doubts. "I'm just now remembering . . . my dad never played with me. Ever. I'd be outside, and he'd never come out." His awareness was growing, the light dawning on his story. "I always wanted a tree fort when I was a boy. But we lived in the city. Then we moved to the country when I was thirteen, and it was awesome. I had all the trees in the world. I built this tree fort. But even though my dad worked in construction, he didn't help me. I sat in it maybe five or six times. My dad never came out. I remember feeling like, *This sucks. Who's here to see this?*" A sad story. Small wonder Sam finds it hard to believe that God wants anything good for him. I said, "I'm so excited about this kayak—I think God is, too." A longer pause, and then Sam spoke for many a man: "It's like you're speaking French to me. I just don't get it."

A simple story, about a kayak. But one I've heard repeated hundreds, perhaps thousands, of times before, in one form or another, from different men at different stages, touching on the same basic doubt in our hearts. Of course, it runs into much deeper waters than buying a kayak, especially when it involves the death of a child, a dream that has died, a life that feels mostly hard and disappointing and not much else. Whatever life has taught us, and though we may not have put it into these exact words, we feel that we are alone. Simply look at the way men live. If I were to give an honest assessment of my life for the past thirty years, I'd have to confess the bulk of it as Striving and Indulging. Pushing myself hard to excel, taking on the battles that come to me with determination but also with a fear-based drivenness, believing deep down inside that there is no one I can trust to come through for me. Striving. And then, arranging for little pleasures along the way to help ease the pain of the drivenness and loneliness. Dinners out, adventure gear. Indulging. A fatherless way to live.

George MacDonald was so right when he said, "The hardest, gladdest thing in the world is to cry *Father!* from a full heart . . . the refusal to look up to God as our father is the one central wrong in the whole human affair; the inability, the one central misery." The one central misery. That's worth thinking about. I didn't used to believe it, really. You see, this fatherlessness has become so normal—*our* normal—we don't even think about it much.

True Sons of a True Father

And that is why Jesus kept coming back to this central issue, over and over, driving at it in his teachings, his parables, his penetrating questions. If you look again, through the lens that most of us feel fundamentally fatherless, I think you'll find it very close indeed to the center of Jesus' mission. "Which of you, if his son asks for bread, will give him a stone? Or if he asks for a fish, will give him a snake?" (Matt. 7:9–10 NIV). Well? We rush ahead to the rest of the passage, but I think Jesus is asking us a real question and he wants a real answer. I expect he paused here, his penetrating, compassionate eyes scanning the listeners before him. Well? I hesitate. I guess you're right. I wouldn't, and apart from the exceptionally wicked man, I can't think of any decent father— even if he is self-absorbed—who would do such a thing. Jesus continues, "If you, then, though you are evil, know how to give good gifts to your children, how much more will your Father in heaven give good gifts to those who ask him!" (v. 11 NIV).

He is trying to speak to our deepest doubt about the universe.

Look at the birds of the air. Consider the lilies in the field. Are you not much more valuable to your true Father than they? (Matt. 6:26, 28). Hmmm. I'm not sure how to answer. I mean, of course, there's the "right" answer. And then there is the wound in our hearts toward fatherhood, and there is also the way our lives have gone. "What do you think? If a man owns a hundred sheep, and one of them wanders away, will he not leave the ninety-nine on the hills and go to look for the one that wandered off?" (Matt. 18:12 NIV). Yet another question, pressing into the submerged fears in our hearts, another question wanting another answer. Well? Wouldn't he? "And if he finds it, I tell you the truth, he is happier about that one sheep than about the ninety-nine that did not wander off. In the same way your Father in heaven is not willing that any of these little ones should be lost" (vv. 13–14 NIV).

Wherever you are in your ability to believe it at this moment in your life, at least you can see what Jesus is driving at. You have a good Father. He is better than you thought. He cares. He really does. He's kind and generous. He's out for your best. This is absolutely central to the teaching of Jesus, though I have to admit, it never really struck a chord in me until I began to think through the need for masculine initiation, and came straight up against the question, *But who will do the initiating?* Most of our fathers are gone, or checked out, or uninitiated men themselves. There are a few men, a very few, who have fathers initiating them in substantive ways. Would that we all were so lucky. And, some guys have found a mentor, but they also are hard to come by. Especially those who understand masculine initiation. So, again, I still find myself wondering, *Where can we find a true father to initiate us?* Then pow—the lights begin to come on. Maybe this is what Jesus was getting at. That is the way of any real discovery—we find ourselves in need, and then the answer that has actually been before us for some time suddenly matters, suddenly makes sense.

In this case—our need for a real father to provide masculine initiation—the need is about as deep as any human need can get. Henri Nouwen came to see, rather late in his life, that this longing was "the deepest yearning of my heart." The longing for a really good father. Tom Wolfe calls it "the deepest search in life."

The deepest search in life, it seemed to me, the thing that in one way or another was central to all living was man's search to find a father, not merely the father of his flesh, not merely the lost father of his youth, but the image of a strength and wisdom external to his need and superior to his hunger, to which the belief and power of his own life could be united. ("The Story of a Novel")

A RADICAL SHIFT

For you did not receive a spirit that makes you a slave again to fear, but you received the Spirit of sonship. And by him we cry, "*Abba*, Father." (Rom. 8:15 NIV)

Because you are sons, God sent the Spirit of his Son into our hearts, the Spirit who calls out, "*Abba*, Father." So you are no longer a slave, but a son; and since you are a son, God has also made you also an heir. (Gal. 4:6–7 NIV)

Most of the men I've counseled over the years understand that Christianity is an offer of forgiveness, made available to us through the sacrifice of Jesus on the cross. They see God the way Balian sees his father at the start of his journey. What they don't seem to grasp is, there is more. That forgiveness was made available to each of us *so that* we might come home to the Father. Forgiveness is not the goal. Coming home to the Father is the goal. So a man who calls himself a Christian, attends church, and has some hope of heaven when he dies has *not* received the lion's share of what God intended him to receive through the work of Christ. He will find himself living still very much alone, stuck in his journey, wondering why he cannot become the man he longs to be.

He has not come into sonship.

Take a closer look at the story of the prodigal son, one of many stories Jesus told to try to get it into our hearts where we stand with the Father, and how he feels about us. Yes, the prodigal went AWOL, ran off to Vegas with the family fortune, blew it all on cheap whores and high-stakes poker. Yes, we have done the same, more or less . . . in most cases, much more than less. But that is not the point of the story. The story is not primarily about the prodigal. It is about the father's heart. "But while he was still a long way off, his father saw him and was filled with compassion for him; he ran to his son, threw his arms around him and kissed him" (Luke 15:20 NIV). This is the kind of Father you have. This is how he feels about you. *This* is the purpose for which Christ came.

> But when the time had fully come, God sent his Son, born of a woman, born under law, to redeem those under law, that we might receive the full rights of sons. Because you are sons, God sent the Spirit of his Son into our hearts, the Spirit who calls out, "*Abba*, Father." So you are no longer a slave, but a son; and since you are a son, God has made you also an heir. (Gal. 4:4–7 NIV)

As George MacDonald explains, "The word used by St. Paul does not imply that God adopts children that are not his own, but rather that a second time he fathers his own, that a second time they are born—this time from above. That he will make himself tenfold, yea, infinitely their father" (*Unspoken Sermons*).

We begin to make the one most central, most essential shift in all the world, the shift Christianity is focused on, by at least beginning with the objective truth. How this plays out in our lives will come later. For now, there are things you must know. You *are* the son of a kind, strong, and engaged Father, a Father wise enough to guide you in the Way, generous enough to provide for your journey. His first act of provision happened before you were even born, when he rescued you through the life, death, and resurrection of our elder brother, Jesus of Nazareth. Then he called you to himself—perhaps is calling you even now—to come home to him through faith in Christ. When a man gives his life to Jesus Christ, when he turns as the prodigal son turned for home and is reconciled to the Father, many remarkable things take place. At the core of them is a coming into true sonship.

Balian had many lessons to learn, much catching up to do from his years of fatherlessness. He was about to get a sort of crash course in the way of the cowboy, and the warrior, and not long after that the lover, so that he might become a king. But first, he had to take the risk, accept the fact that his father had come for him.

THE FATHER IS INITIATING HIS SONS

"I'll never find him out there." I had returned home from a day of fishing, alone, on one of my favorite rivers. But I was agitated, irritated, pacing around the family room, and I couldn't have told you why. It wasn't that I hadn't caught any fish. Something else was eating at me. Stasi asked, "Honey, what's wrong?" "I don't know," I said, slumping down on a chair. A long moment of silence, and then this sentence: "I'll never find him out there." "Him" was my father. My confession took me by surprise. I had no idea that I had been looking for my father, all those years, out on the rivers and lakes, rod in hand. For that was the only time in my life I ever really had my dad. But those days have been gone some thirty years now, and will never return. What am I to do?

I don't want to live fatherless anymore.

You see, we need fathering still. All of us. More than we know. There are many places in us yet orphaned, many places that need initiation into manhood. This is as true of the seventy-year-old man as it is of the sixteen-year-old boy. We are Unfinished Men. And in truth, the Father has been fathering us for a long time now or, at least, trying to. What I'm suggesting is a new way of looking at your life as a man. To see your life as a process of initiation into masculine maturity, and your Father doing the initiating. Invited, like Balian, on a journey by your true Father.

We are Unfinished Men. Hebrews says that God is about finishing his work in us. Again, MacDonald explains what our Father is up to:

> He will have them share in his being and nature—strong wherein he cares for strength; tender and gracious as he is tender and gracious; angry as and where he is angry. Even in the small matter

of power, he will have them able to do whatever his Son Jesus could on the earth, whose life was the life of the perfect man, whose works were those of perfected humanity ... when we come to think with him, when the mind of the son is as the mind of the father, the action of the son the same as that of the father, then is the son *of* the father, then are we the sons of God.

None but a child could become a son; the idea is, a spiritual coming of age; *only when the child is a man is he really and fully a son.* (*Unspoken Sermons*)

Our Father has come for us, and our initiation is under way. It can now proceed with even greater clarity and intimacy. The horizon has opened before us. It is a risky venture, to be sure, this realignment of our view of life as masculine initiation, this turning to God as Father. But I know of few other truths that can bring a man such hope as this.

Father, okay. Okay. I don't know how much of this I believe, but I know this—I need a father. There is so much in me that yet needs fathering. And I don't want to live fatherless anymore. So come to me, and help me make the shift. You have taken me home, through Christ, to be your own son. I accept that. I give my life back to you, to be your true son. Father me. Father me.

3 Boyhood

Keep me as the apple of your eye.
—Psalm 17:8 niv

When I was a boy, my father worked as a traveling salesman, in paper goods and then garden supplies. I was his only son, with two older sisters, and come summertime Dad would take me along with him as he called on accounts across the western states—Oregon, Idaho, Colorado, Wyoming, Montana. It was a time of great adventures. Together. I was his navigator, poring over the road maps, which in those days you could get for free at any gas station. (They pumped your gas and checked your oil then, too—how many of you remember that?) My dad loved to fish, and as the weekend drew near he'd plan the route so as to land us near a lake or stream. We'd camp for the weekend, and fish to our hearts' content. Meaning, sunup to sundown. He'd make us fried-egg sandwiches for dinner, or sometimes Spam,

37

which I loved. We slept in a tent. And if we didn't catch anything, Dad would swing me by Happy Jack's Fish Farm to make sure I landed a few. (It was decades later, as a father myself, that I learned you actually *pay* for the fish you catch there.)

Summertime to a boy seems eternal. Echoes of the endless days of wonder in Eden. It seemed to me that we'd be on the road for months and months, just me and him, sleeping at the Roadway or the Holiday Inn or, better, little places like Moe's Alpine Chalet Cabins with a creek running right behind them. No homework. No chores. We'd eat at the A&W (we both loved root beer). We were rock hounds then, too, pulling into every little nook to search for snowflake obsidian and geodes called thunder eggs. After what seemed like six months of "travels with my father," Dad would make the loop back home and pass through eastern Oregon, to his father's cattle ranch, where I would be dropped off for the rest of the summer.

In the time of my boyhood, the ranch was a place of unending adventures. Later, it would become a key place for the raising of the cowboy. My grandfather had horses and cattle, barns and tractors, and a yard with a huge lawn that seemed to go on forever. There was a pond nestled back in one of the pastures on the property, a small pond half filled with cattails, a place of mystery and delight to a boy. There were bullfrogs there, and sometimes a great blue heron, standing so utterly still, like a lamppost, waiting to seize an unfortunate catfish. There must have been hundreds of fish in that little pond—too many in fact, for they never grew much past seven or eight inches long—but size didn't matter to me. It was abundance I was after. I'd dig for red worms in the soft, moist earth lining the irrigation ditch by the house, and carry them in an old Folgers coffee can to the pond, where I would fish with a hook and bobber. I loved watching those old red and white bobbers, sitting nearly motionless on the surface, waiting for it to tug, tug, tug then plunge beneath the surface, letting me know my prize was on the line.

> And once below a time I lordly had the trees and leaves
>> Trail with daisies and barley
>> Down the rivers of the windfall light.
> And as I was green and carefree, famous among the barns
> About the happy yard and singing as the farm was home,
>> In the sun that is young once only,
>> Time let me play and be
>> Golden in the mercy of his means,
> And green and golden I was huntsman and herdsman, the calves
> Sang to my horn, the foxes on the hills barked clear and cold,
>> And the sabbath rang slowly
>> In the pebbles of the holy streams. (Dylan Thomas, "Fern Hill")

A WORLD THAT IS SAFE

We begin our journey into sonship by looking backward, to what our lives as boys were like, and, more important, what they were *meant* to be. For so much of the way we now approach life as men was set in motion in our youth—some of it for good, and some not so good. We want to recover what was good, and find healing for all that was not.

Boyhood is a time of exploration and wonder, and to be a boy is to be an explorer, from the time when the little guy figures out how to crawl up the stairs (he is gone in a flash), to the time he discovers that if he jumps over the back fence he can get down to Jimmy's house, where they have a secret fort. When God set Adam in the Garden of Eden, he set his son in a world that was, at the very same moment, safe and secure yet full of mystery and adventure. There was no reason whatsoever to be afraid, and every reason to dare. As Mark Twain said, "There comes a time in every rightly constructed boy's life when he has a raging desire to go somewhere and dig for hidden treasure." (How many of you, when you were a boy, thought there was treasure buried somewhere in the yard, or stowed away in your grandparents' attic?) Evil is—for now—held at bay. Such is the world God intended for the boy. And that world is created under the sheltering strength of a father who makes you feel safe.

For this is the time in life when we were meant to come into the knowledge that we are the beloved son, the apple of our father's eye.

My friend Bart, whose brother is four years older, once told me, "Growing up, I felt I always lived in my brother's shadow." For the elder was a better athlete, and Bart always felt that it was his brother who had his father's delight.

But there was a period early on in my life when my brother went off to school, and I hadn't yet—I think I was four or five, and I spent all my days with my father on the family farm. I had two years with my dad, all to myself. He'd get me up in the morning and take me with him. I remember the tractor—this was back in the early fifties and they didn't have the big cab then like they do now—you rode out in the open, all those moving parts thrashing around, which just fascinated me as a boy. A little fearful to me, yet I felt so safe between the legs of my father. Holding on to the steering wheel, he'd make me think I was really driving this big, powerful piece of machinery.

They lived in west Texas, and Bart recalls a time when they were visiting his uncle's farm about twenty miles away when tornado warnings came in. "His family was pulling mattresses down into the storm cellar, getting ready to ride it out, and they urged us to stay. But my dad wanted to get home to my mom and brother." While they drove the back roads home, they saw a twister heading across the plains about a mile away. "My dad took me out and held me in his arms as we sat on the fender of the pickup and watched this tornado just destroy the town of Cotton Center, Texas. He put his arms around me, and just being in the arms of my father, I felt so safe."

Safe in your father's arms—*that* is what it feels like to be the beloved son.

During summers at the ranch, I slept in the basement, in a

huge, sagging old bed with a brass headboard and a white chenille comforter. I was certain there were treasures down there, too, somewhere in the rows of jars of my grandmother's canning—peaches, apricots, beans, jams. It had a moist, dank coolness that was wonderful when the August days reached into the hundreds. But some nights—when the big thunderstorms would roll through, rattling the windows in the old house—it wasn't wonderful at all. I was scared, and my grandfather's bedroom seemed so far away. I would hide beneath the covers until I built up enough courage and adrenaline to dare the dash upstairs to climb into bed with my grandfather. There, I could fall asleep again. Safe in the presence of a man I knew could handle anything in the world.

There is a remarkable picture of this sense of safety and security a father gives his son in the Italian movie *Life Is Beautiful*. The story is set in WWII. The boy is perhaps five years old, son of a Jewish father and an Italian mother. When his family is taken away to a concentration camp, the father hides his son among the men being taken to the all-male camp so that he will not be separated from the boy, and so that he might protect him. For many months in the camp, the father shields the son from the enemy, and the ruthless evil around them. There, in the midst of darkness, the boy shows a stunning immunity to it all, trusting fully in the goodness of his father, playing the endless games they make up together.

The safety that a father's strength provides allows a boy to *be* a boy, creates the universe for a boy's heart to come fully alive. For a number of years Stasi and I raised our boys in a house with a second story. I think there were maybe thirteen stairs leading to the upper level. Often in the evenings, just before bedtime, the boys in their jammies with feet in them, we would play a game where they would get as far back on the landing as they could, get a running start to leap off the stairs, and fly through the air into my arms below. I was blown away by their trust in me, such abandoned confidence. When a boy has this confidence, this security and safety created by masculine strength over him, the whole world opens before him. He is able to live *as a boy*—an explorer and adventurer.

A WORLD OF ADVENTURES AND BATTLES

After the game of leaping off the stairs came bedtime, and a ritual. "Once upon a time there were three cowboys named Samuel, Blaine, and Luke, and they lived on a ranch near Colorado Springs . . ." I'd lie on the floor in their shared bedroom and make up stories about buffalo hunts, or rescuing someone from the Indians, or a great adventure they would take to catch wild horses in a box canyon. This is what the heart of a boy longs for—daring adventures, battles, uncharted territory to be discovered. Spend an afternoon watching boys at play, and you will see something of what God intended when he created man *as a man*, when he created maleness, masculinity.

Luke found an old skateboard and took off the wheels and "trucks," leaving only the deck. Then he went off to find an old pair of sneakers and some duct tape. "Dad, can I use these?" "For what?" "For a trick I want to do." "Sure." Using generous amounts of tape, he strapped the shoes to the deck or vice versa, and now he's bouncing on the trampoline and doing snowboarding tricks—back flips and the like, with this board strapped to his feet. A classic moment around this house. We have a trampoline, sure, but how can we take it to the next level? How can we make this an adventure? A question that comes as natural to a boy as breathing.

In my very early years, before I turned six, we lived in the suburbs then sprouting east of San Francisco, acres and acres of ranch-style houses built for the post-WWII couples now raising their families. Palo Alto was the edge of the boom, and there were many open lots and fields yet undeveloped where my buddies and I would explore for hours and hours. Wild anise grew there, tasting of licorice. We'd pick it and chew on it as we adventured through the fields. As boys will always do, we found a way down into one of the drainage ditches, a concrete canal for what was once a creek flowing through fields and forests of California oak. (A hole in a fence is an *invitation* to a boy, a challenge even—what lies beyond?) There were pollywogs down in the pools of water, and we'd catch them with our bare hands and put the wiggly little critters into mayonnaise jars full of murky water, take them home to watch them sprout legs, lose their tails, turn into frogs.

Many of the adventures of boyhood come in the form of books. I had favorite books like *The Adventures of Jerry Muskrat*, *The Wind in the Willows*, and *Farewell to Shady Glade*. My boys have loved the Redwall series, animals living high adventures and fighting great battles. Which reminds us that the boy is also a *warrior*, and all those games he plays and battles he imagines are preparation for the day he enters the stage of the warrior in its fullness. When a boy imagines himself as a character, it is nearly always a superhero of some sort. I remember my sixth birthday. It was June 6, 1966. I woke to find balloons in my room, and a string leading out my bedroom door, down the hall, into the washroom, back out again, down another hall—a treasure hunt. At the end of the trail lay a box, and in that box was my heart's desire: a Batman costume. I was thrilled. I put that costume on and didn't take it off for a week, running around the house, leaping off sofas, charging through houseplants, all the while singing the theme song to the show.

A boy wants to be *powerful*. That's what's behind the superhero thing. To be powerful, and dangerous, a force to be reckoned with—that is the heart of the warrior emerging.

I think the first sounds my sons learned to make were of explosions, followed shortly by machine guns, bazookas, and other powerful weapons. This comes for most boys before learning to talk. Picture a little guy, cheeks puffed out, a bit of drool coming down, making *k-boom, k-boom* and *kertch-kertch-kercth* sounds. It's a gift, really, a talent boys have been given by God, though when a girl does it she sounds silly. I was asking my boys just the other day what some of the best aspects of their boyhood have been. The first thing out of their mouths was, "The weapons we'd make, all the games we'd play."

We went to Disneyland when Blaine was maybe eight, and all

day long he kept talking about the Daniel Boone flintlock rifle he would buy in Frontier Village. We asked him to wait till the end of the evening, because it's rather hard to go on a roller coaster holding a four-foot-long toy musket. But we ended up breaking down and buying it around 3:00 p.m. because he wouldn't stop talking about it.

That gun has gone through several generations of development. After the season of pioneers and cowboys gave way to the modern warfare of SEALs and snipers, Blaine painted it black, including a piece of PVC pipe he screwed on to the barrel for a scope. That gun is still in action. I used it myself, last night, sneaking up on the boys while they were doing homework. *Kertch-kertch-kertch.* Which, of course, ended homework for about half an hour because I had declared war and they—like any boys—had to answer the call.

A WORLD OF SURPRISES

There's a touching story a man told me about a ritual that would take place every evening when his father got home. The father would change out of his work clothes—a business suit—and into his "house clothes," and the children would get to dig deep into his pockets for whatever "treasures" they might find in his work trousers—a quarter, a pen, a cuff link, a stick of gum. The treasures were theirs to keep. So Daddy coming home was always an event that brought excitement and anticipation. Which is a wonderful thing to have linked with fatherhood, especially as we make the connection to God as Father, from whom, the Scriptures say, comes "every good and perfect gift" (James 1:17 NIV).

If you think again of the films and stories that portray the stages, you will see this plays a central role in the son coming to understand how much his father adores him. Balian is given gifts by his father—a sword, and his father's ring, which entitles him to his estate—gifts that help Balian believe he *is* his son. Frodo is given gifts by Bilbo, his uncle by birth but his father in truth.

On the morning of the last day Frodo was alone with Bilbo, and the old hobbit pulled out from under his bed a wooden box.... He took from the box a small sword in an old shabby leathern scabbard. Then he drew it, and its polished and well-tended blade glittered suddenly, cold and bright. "This is Sting," he said, and thrust it with little effort deep into a wooden beam. "Take it, if you like ... also there is this!" said Bilbo, bringing out a parcel which seemed to be rather heavy for its size. He unwound several folds of old cloth, and held up a small shirt of mail. It was close woven of many rings, as supple almost as linen, cold as ice, and harder than steel. With it was a belt of pearl and crystal. "It's a pretty thing, isn't it?" said Bilbo, moving it in the light. "And useful. It is my dwarf mail that Thorin gave me." (*The Fellowship of the Ring*)

Those gifts end up saving Frodo's life.

A few of us were talking about our fathers the other night, and sharing some of the good memories we have of them. Morgan told us of something like the story I just recounted that pertained to his father, who had a ritual of a poker game each week. The kids would be sent to bed long before their father got home, but the next morning they'd wake to find his winnings on the kitchen table, divided into piles for each of his children to take as their own. Treasure. Booty. For no other reason than "you are my beloved sons and daughters." Gary then remembered a time when he was very young, and his father told him, "After you take a nap, when you wake up I have a surprise for you." He had put up a rope swing for Gary, hanging from the tree in the front yard. "I felt like he was thinking of me, wanted me to be happy." This, too, lays a foundation in the heart of the boy, for he comes to learn that life is not something you have to arrange for. There is someone who cares, someone who wants to give you good gifts. Think of Joseph's special, beautiful coat. The young man I told you about, Sam, would not be doubting about the kayak if his father had given treasures to him when he was young.

My grandfather had long quit smoking by the time I knew him, and he had taken up a love for butterscotch LifeSavers as a sort of substitute. He always carried a roll of them in the glove box of his pickup, and we'd be rolling down the road and he'd flip open the box and ask me, "Cigarette?" I loved it, love butterscotch LifeSavers to this day. There was an old caretaker who lived on the ranch, a crusty old cowboy named Bill who lived in a trailer out by the horses. One summer afternoon Bill—who'd taken a liking to me—called me over to his trailer and said, "I've got something for you." He reached in his pocket and pulled out an old pocket-knife, his own, worn from years of ranch work, and handed it to me. What a treasure that was, for a boy with his very own pocket-knife is a boy with endless possibilities before him. That small gift made my summer.

BELOVED SON

It's experiences like these that speak to the heart of a boy. *You are noticed. Your heart matters. Your father adores you.* For we must remember that above all else, boyhood is the time of Affirmation, the time when a boy comes to learn and learn deeply that he *is* the beloved son.

I explained in *Wild at Heart* that every man and every boy is asking one core question: "Do I have what it takes?" It's why, when the boys ride their bikes with no hands, or learn to do a backflip on the trampoline, they want me there to *see* it. And all that crazy stuff young men do—cliff jumping into the river, riding motor-cycles, all the competition of sports—that is fueled by the same drive. That is the expression of a man's need for validation. *Do I have what it takes?* is a core question to be sure, and I still hold that it is the vital question of the masculine journey. But there is a deeper and prior need, one that comes first—in this stage—and one that must be met first, or the boy cannot move with confi-dence into any of the other stages.

A boy yearns to know that he is prized.

This is more than just being loved in a generic sort of way. "Of course I love you—you're my son." A boy can see right through anything false in that. He yearns to know he is *adored*. *Uniquely*. That he holds a special place in his father's heart, a place no one and nothing else can rival. Without this certainty down in the core of his being, the boy will misinterpret the stages and lessons that are to come, for as a young man (cowboy) he will soon be tested, and he will face battles and challenges as a warrior, and those tests and challenges often feel to men like a form of rejection or coldheartedness on the part of God, because he does not first know in his heart of hearts that he *is* the beloved son. The son of my right hand, as Benjamin was called; or the son of my delight, as surely Joseph knew; or my beloved son in whom I am so pleased, as the Father said of Jesus.

Without this bedrock of affirmation, this core of assurance, a man will move unsteadily through the rest of his life, trying to prove his worth and earn belovedness through performance or achievement, through sex, or in a thousand other ways. Quite often he doesn't know this is his search. He simply finds himself uncertain in some core place inside, ruled by fears and the opinions of others, yearning for someone to notice him. He longs for comfort, and it makes him uneasy because at thirty-seven or fifty-one shouldn't he be beyond that now? A young place in his heart is yearning for something never received.

Those road trips with my father across the West, all those times together in a boat out on a lake, or looking for rocks, stopping for a soda, all that time my dad gave to me and me alone—that was the greatest gift of affirmation he ever gave. It wasn't grudging. It wasn't because he had to, or ought to. He *wanted* to be with me. He enjoyed it. He wanted me with him. He prized me. I never questioned that, at least, not when I was young.

Now, yes, a mother plays a crucial role in a boy's life. From her a boy learns mercy, tenderness, and unconditional love. Who did you run to when you scraped your knee? Who would you rather have told that you got in trouble at school—Mom or Dad? Dad typically administrates justice, and Mom offers mercy. But in a core way that is essential to the masculine journey, the bestowing of the mantle of beloved son needs to come from the father. That father might be a man other than your biological father, a man who is father to you in truer ways. Paul calls Timothy his beloved son, and you can imagine it meant the world to his young apprentice (1 Cor. 4:17; 2 Tim. 1:2).

My grandfather fathered me, too, in some very important ways. He called me "Johnny," and he was the only one ever to call me that. Oh, how I loved those summers at the ranch. We'd wake early in the morning and head down to the small diner in town for coffee and milk and donuts. Nina's Diner was the gathering place for ranchers, seated along the counter, swapping information about the weather or cattle prices. My grandfather would set me right there beside him, right in the action, at his side. I was proud he was my "Pop" and I could tell he was proud I was his grandson, his Johnny. I was prized by a man I loved. This is the greatest gift any boy ever receives.

Come back for a moment to Jesus' probing questions regarding our feelings about God as Father. He almost seems puzzled.

"Are you not much more valuable than they? Will he not leave the ninety-nine on the hills and go off to look for the one that wandered off? How much more will your Father in heaven give good gifts to those who ask him!" In other words, don't you know how your Father feels about you? Jesus did. He walked through the world knowing he was the beloved son, the favored One. It's what enabled him to live as he did. As Jan Bovenmars wrote:

> Jesus had the Heart of a Son . . . *knew* himself to be the Son, felt very much like a [Beloved] Son, looked on God as "Abba," his dear Father, lived in a Father-Son relationship. The divine relationship Son-Father filled his human heart; it was his secret, his joy; a constant awareness; a basic attitude that determined his behavior. (*A Biblical Spirituality of the Heart*)

This relationship was meant to be our secret, our joy also. We were meant to *know* this too. First through our earthly fathers, and then, by the extension of fatherhood, to our Father in the heavens. But few there are who came through their boyhood with such knowledge intact, without a trace of doubt.

WOUNDED

Sometime in elementary school, I can't remember exactly when, for the years have mingled memories and blurred events, it might have been around fourth or fifth grade, something went wrong in the world. My father began to disappear. His story is too long to tell here, but through a series of setbacks and disappointments, a successive loss of jobs, he began to drink. And his drinking got hold of him, like a riptide gets hold of your legs even in shallow water, and pulls you under. In his alcoholism, he began to retreat from us, gone, but not to work, just gone, sometimes spending hours out in his workshop alone, drinking and doing crossword puzzles. Dragged out to sea. It was the beginning of the collapse of my family.

The summer trips came to an end. The fishing came to an end. Mom had to go to work. I went to Boy Scouts alone, came home to an empty house. I felt abandoned. My world ceased to be a safe place. Emotionally, physically, spiritually, I became an orphan. And a terrible lie settled deep into my heart: *you are on your own.* A boy without a father, in a dangerous world. The days of the beloved son cut off, and I never knew why. Perhaps it was something I did. Perhaps I could have prevented it.

The crucial thing about the stage of the beloved son—any of the stages, for that matter—is that it not be cut short, assaulted, unfinished, stolen in any way. We were designed to experience belovedness and boyhood, soak in it *for years*, learn its lessons, have them written indelibly upon our hearts, and then pass through this stage to the next, carrying all its treasures with us. We were meant to move on *with the help of our fathers*, into the next stage of masculine initiation.

Alas. Name those men you know who did.

Far more often than not this stage *is* stolen. How quickly do betrayal and slavery fall upon Joseph after his father gives him the coat of many colors, the symbol of his delight. We don't know exactly how much time has passed, but those events are told in the same chapter in Genesis, barely verses apart. The result is a stark contrast, the time of being the beloved son cut short by a betrayal.

A boy's heart is wounded in many ways. He is wounded when he does not live in a world made safe by his father, when he is not free to explore and dare and simply *be* a boy, when he is forced to grow up too soon. He is wounded when he *does* have that world, but it ends with a sudden loss of innocence. And most especially, a boy is wounded to the core when he does not know that he *is* the beloved son. Sometimes the wounding is intentional, oftentimes it is not, but this is the story of many a boy, and many a man reading this book, living in the world we have, so far from the Garden.

I remember a young man I counseled years ago—he was bright and gifted, but also far too serious, and driven. A perfectionist. When he was twelve his father left, walked out the door never to return, and the boy needed to go to work to help make ends meet. He cut the grass for neighbors, found odd jobs to do after school. Summers he worked as a lifeguard at the local pool. He told me he never got to play during the summer, never went out for ice cream with his friends, never joined them all when they went down to the swimming hole. But he made Eagle Scout, got excellent grades, worked hard. And no one saw the tragedy of it all. A boy trying to play the man, the world on his shoulders.

You don't want to force the boy to grow up too soon. This is the theme of the beautiful movie *Finding Neverland*, in which a boy is robbed of his boyhood through the illness and death of his mother. The boy becomes "mature," meaning, he shuts his heart away so that it will not be hurt again, and he acts grown-up. Frederick Buechner describes the effects of a boy required to be a man far too early in life in photos he saw of his own father:

> Even in pictures of him as a small boy, he looks harried, seldom if ever smiling, as though he knew that as soon as the shutter snapped, it would all begin again—my grandmother saddling him with more, I suspect, than a small boy's share of her own dark burdens, his younger brothers and sisters looking to him for some kind of strength, some kind of stability, which he must have had to dig deep into himself to find, having barely enough at that age, I can only imagine, to get by on himself. (*The Sacred Journey*)

A couple of months ago, a few men I am closest to were sitting around a fire one evening, talking about our dreams for our lives. The subject on the table was, "What is the life you want to live?" It wasn't a conversation about yachts and the Bahamas. We were talking about finding God's purpose for our lives, wanting to live the life we were created to live. Craig in particular had a hard time going there. As we gently pushed into his reluctance, he admitted, "I just don't believe anything good ever really comes true." A core belief, he'll tell you, one that has shaped his life since he was eight years old. And there is a story with that as well. His father was killed in combat when Craig was seven or eight months old, a fact Craig learned about one afternoon when as a boy of eight his mother and the man he thought was his father sat him down in the living room and told him, "This man you call Dad is not your father. Your real father was killed in combat. This is your stepfather."

"I remember everything about the room that day—the way the couch looked, the parakeet in the corner. Time had stopped. Looking back, I can see that was the turning point in my life. In some horrible way the defining point. I died then." A sudden loss of innocence, a boy's world sent careening off its orbit, sometimes never to be recovered.

Finally, there is the wound that comes when the boy knows very well he is *not* the beloved son. Just this weekend I was talking to a man who at the age of fifty-five is now coming to see this. His parents were missionaries in South America, his father gone most of the time on "church business." "I felt as though they [the Bolivian people] were more important to him than I was. He never played with me, was rarely home. I always felt like, if my father had a picture of a boy in his wallet, it would be a Bolivian boy." He never, ever felt prized by his father. To this day this man struggles with turning to God as a good and loving Father. "Because he took my dad away."

This sort of rejection can be subtle, hidden by a father busy about "more important matters," or simply by a dad who is checked out. A friend of mine told me about all the nights he would sit outside his father's study, the door shut from within. His father was a driven man, a workaholic, and hadn't any time or affection to offer the boy. Through tears he described sitting outside his father's door as a boy of nine or ten, writing little notes and passing them to his father under the door, hoping a note might come back through for him. None ever did. Not one. Ever. The message was clear: "You are not prized. I don't care a bit about you. You are not now, nor ever will be, my beloved son."

And then there are the violent stories, the boys raped by their fathers or beaten by them. The boys who endured years of emotional abuse, being yelled at night after night, "You are a worthless piece of crap." Whatever the details of the story might be, the boy is robbed both of his father and of the deep and fundamental blessing that he is the beloved son. It is the evil one's first and most devastating blow against the soul of a man.

The Evil Behind All Evil

In the mythic story of *The Lion King*, the lion cub Simba is separated in his youth from his father through a murder engineered by his uncle, Scar, the character symbolizing the evil one in our story. Scar arranges for the cub to be caught in a stampede of wildebeests, knowing that his father, Mufasa, will risk his life to save his son. He does, and Simba is saved, but Mufasa is killed. Scar then turns on Simba and accuses him, at such a vulnerable and desperate moment, of causing his father's death. Brokenhearted, frightened, racked with guilt, Simba runs away from home.

This is the enemy's one central purpose—to separate us from

the Father. He uses neglect to whisper, *You see—no one cares. You're not worth caring about.* He uses a sudden loss of innocence to whisper, *This is a dangerous world, and you are alone. You've been abandoned.* He uses assaults and abuses to scream at a boy, *This is all you are good for.* And in this way he makes it nearly impossible for us to know what Jesus knew, makes it so very, very hard to come home to the Father's heart toward us. The details of each story are unique to the boy, but the effect is always a wound in the soul, and with it separation from and suspicion of the Father.

It's been very effective.

But God is not willing to simply let that be the end of the story. Not in any man's life. Remember what Jesus taught us about the Father's heart in the parable of the lost son: "But while he was still a long way off, his father saw him and was filled with compassion for him; he ran to his son, threw his arms around him and kissed him" (Luke 15:20 NIV). Filled with compassion, our Father God will come like a loving Father, and take us close to his heart. He will also take us back to heal the wounds, finish things that didn't get finished. He will come for the boy, no matter how old he might now be, and make him his beloved son. So it might be good to pray at this point:

> Father, what did I miss here, in this stage? Did I know I was the
> beloved son? Do I believe it even now? Come to me, in this place,
> over these years. Speak to me. Do I believe you want good things

for me? Is my heart secure in your love? How was my young heart wounded in my life as a boy? And Jesus, you who came to heal the broken heart, come to me here. Heal this stage in my heart. Restore me as the beloved son. Father me.

RAISING THE BELOVED SON

Permit me to connect a few of the dots from my story. You'll recall those summertime trips with my father, all those hours of fishing together, and how it spoke to me so clearly, *You are the beloved son.* You see now how devastating it was when in fourth or fifth grade my world came to an end. I lost my father, and the fishing trips ended. I think in some ways I felt the loss even more because I *did* have my father's delight, for a time, and then he was taken from me. Back in chapter 1, I told you how I wanted to become a fly fisherman, and recounted the story about the guide who "fathered" me on the South Platte. Can you understand now why that event was so significant for me? It spoke right to the wound. God didn't arrange for tennis lessons. He arranged for a fishing trip. I'm curious—how would that look for you? Perhaps fishing is far from your heart's desire, but how *would* you love to be fathered these days?

Oh! Ephraim is my dear, dear son,
  my child in whom I take pleasure!
Every time I mention his name,
  my heart bursts with longing for him!

Everything in me cries out for him.

Softly and tenderly I wait for him. (Jer. 31:20 MSG)

Put your own name in this verse, in the place of "Ephraim" (a name for God's people, and that includes you). Imagine that God's heart bursts with longing for you. This is the message of Jesus: there is a good and loving Father who cares so deeply and passionately for you. He yearns to be your Father now. He will draw near, if you'll let him. No matter how old we are, our true Father wants us to experience being his beloved sons, and all the joys of boyhood that go with it. But it requires opening our hearts, which will take us back into some of our deepest wounds, and the cynicism and resignation that shut our hearts down a long time ago. God does this so that he might bring his love and healing to the fatherless boy within us, the boy that still needs to know he is the beloved son.

And so, to begin with, you might ask yourself, "Did I have a father with whom I felt safe?" and, "Did I know I was prized by my father?" "Was I invited to be a boy, did I get to live a boy's life as it was meant to be?" You might even want to write out your answers to those questions, especially the follow-up question, "Why . . . or why not?" Tell your story, at least to yourself, and to God.

The Father will do many things to try to get us back to this longing in our hearts—the longing for a father, the longing to be prized, to be the beloved son. All it takes for me is the movie *A River Runs Through It*. He might haunt you through a story far too similar to your own, a story that somehow tells you about yourself. That happened for a friend named Paul who came to one of our retreats, when he watched a scene we showed from *Good Will Hunting*. In truth, Paul was about to bail out of the event. It was stirring too much in him, and he wanted out. He was headed for the back door when the clip came on where Will is finally facing the wound of being physically abused by his foster father, and Paul sat down on the steps and began to weep. For that was his story, too. The Father had captured him, brought his wounded heart up from the depths of his soul, so that he might grieve and also that he might open this place in his heart to God. Paul became a Christian that day.

Think about what you love, and what you longed for as a boy. When my friend Gary was a boy, his father gave him a "Rifleman" rifle, a toy based on the old Chuck Connors Western. "It was my favorite toy," he said. But a neighborhood bully broke it, simply took it out of Gary's hands and whacked it against a tree. "I think that's when I started to mistrust people," Gary said. Forty years later, last Christmas, Gary's family gave him a real 30/30. He has recovered a love for guns, and the Father has been fathering him in this intimate way. Gary will often go up to the shooting range all by himself, just with his rifle, to be with God.

Curtis is a young friend of mine who not too long ago became an attorney. Shortly after that he also became a father. His nights were just as busy as his days and he knew he was in need of some time just for his heart. "Curtis, what was it you used to love as a boy?" I asked. "Baseball," he said. He played all the time, but life eventually edged it out, and a love of his heart seemed gone forever. Like most men, he just assumed that was that. It's gone. I ran into him maybe six months later in a meeting, and afterward he asked if he might have a word with me. "This is huge," he said. "I asked God what he had for me, and he said 'Baseball.' It felt crazy, but I looked into a local league and found that they needed a player. It's been the best thing I've done in a long time!" He relayed all this with a big smile on his face.

The heart of the boy can be resurrected, and no matter what our age is now, we can *know* that we are prized, that we have a place in our Father's heart that no one and nothing else can rival. We *are* his beloved sons, and we can begin to experience that in deeply personal ways.

Father, I need to know that I am your son, and that there is a place for me in your heart that no one else can fill. I need to experience your love. Raise the orphaned boy in me. Take me back to those places where I felt so missed, and show me that my heart matters to you. Give me eyes to see and ears to hear how you are raising the heart of the boy in me, raising me in belovedness even now. Heal and restore my soul as a son—as your beloved son. Give me the grace to believe it.

4   Cowboy

And [the boy] grew in wisdom and stature,
and in favor with God and men.

—Luke 2:52 niv

In the northwestern corner of Wyoming, just below the far more popular (and crowded) Yellowstone National Park, lies a range of mountains arguably the most dramatic and beautiful of any in North America. Thrust up by the collision of two massive blocks of the earth's crust, the Tetons rise abruptly, heaving violently from the valley floor like a great fortress wall, crowned with jagged edges and spires. The highest is the Grand, 13,770 feet above sea level and one of the classic mountaineering peaks in the world. On August 1, 2002, we found ourselves high on a southern ridge, in the early morning light, attempting the summit. Named for Glenn Exum, the man who first ascended it— alone and without protection—the Exum ridge is "undeniably one of the most spectacular routes of its grade anywhere in the world" as the guide service has it, with "sensational exposure." Meaning, there are places on the ridge where the drop is two thousand feet or more.

There were eight of us on the ridge, roped together in two teams—my son Samuel (thirteen at the time) and me, Morgan, and our guide. Then Gary and his son Jesse (fifteen), and another young man, Aaron, led by their guide. We climbed the Grand in two teams of four, using a hip belay. In a hip belay the lead climber ascends to a ledge or shelf or some place he can stand—or better, sit, his legs braced in front of him against rock so that should his buddy below take a fall he won't be yanked off the mountain himself. It's a choice made in favor of speed, being faster than using various climbing gear to set and then remove fixed protection at every belay station. And speed is one of the nonnegotiables on the Grand. You want to get up and off the peak before there are any signs of the afternoon thunderstorms so common to the West, which bring with them deadly lightning strikes. The following summer, one climber was killed and several others critically burned by lightning on the Exum Ridge, right about where we were ascending.

Once you commit to the ridge there is no turning back, no down-climbing options available. The only way off is up. The faster the better. It adds to the drama of the climb, facing each tough move with no choice but to do it. Several times I would make a move or climb a section of a pitch and think to myself, *I hope Sam can do this—he's never made a move like that before.* We'd done quite a bit of climbing, stuff much harder than the actual moves on the Grand, except for the thousands of feet of exposure on three sides. There was no one to coach him up, and no communication between us except tugs on the rope to signal "Ready to belay—you can start climbing" and "Okay, I'm climbing." Eighty to a hundred feet or so of rope lies between, and with the arc of the ridge sweeping ever upward, you cannot see the climbers above or below until you are nearly upon them, or they upon you.

The expedition was planned as a part of Samuel's "Vision Quest," a year devoted to his passage from beloved son into young manhood—into the stage of the cowboy. (I'll tell you more about Sam's initiation in a coming chapter.) But what happened was, it proved to be crucial to every one of our hearts, for every one of us was yet in need of fathering here, in adventure, into a strength and courage we doubted we possessed but desperately wanted to know we had. So I would take my position, signal Sam to climb, and hope and pray that he made each move as I took in the rope that signaled his ascent. My favorite snapshots, most of which are captured in my mind, are of those moments when Sam would appear, big smile on his face, making his approach to my current belay station. We'd trade a quick high five and a word of encouragement, and usually by then Morgan was tugging on my end of his rope to say, "Get going."

ADVENTURE

I would set the beginning of the cowboy (or ranger) stage in early adolescence—around age twelve or thirteen—and suggest it carries into the midtwenties. Though I would be quick to remind you that the stages overlap. What little tike doesn't want adventure, as he races his sled down a hill or learns to climb a tree? What man of fifty doesn't need time away, in the outdoors? But a notable shift begins to take place in the boy's soul as he approaches his teens, a yearning for *real* adventure. Something inside tells him that he needs to prove himself, needs to be tested. He wants to learn how to do things—how to drive a car, to hunt birds, to build a loft in his room. And now the Question of a man's soul begins to present itself in nearly everything the boy-becoming-a-young-man does: *Do I have what it takes?* In the cowboy stage the answer comes partly through adventure, and partly through hard work.

For as long as I can remember growing up, I sucked at sports. Never once got picked in elementary school when they were choosing teams for kickball. I was part of the group of "leftovers" who were sort of divvied up between the team captains as a concession. What does that teach a boy about himself? And when I went out for basketball in middle school, I only made the B team and spent all my time there on the bench. I struck out every time I tried to play baseball, was too slow to ever qualify for the track team. It was humiliating. All my friends were athletes, and I soon found myself on the outside looking in. I just didn't have the gifts my friends seemed to have—which can be overcome if a boy has determination, and a coach—but my dad was checked out at this point so I didn't have anyone to coach me along. It was an immense source of shame for me. I quit trying in eighth grade, and never attempted a team sport again.

But there was a craving in me for adventure and testing, and I found what my soul needed at my grandfather's ranch and in the mountains. At the ranch I learned to saddle and ride horses, and herd cattle—something none of my city friends knew how to do—and it gave my heart a strength and assurance I desperately needed. I'll never forget the first day I galloped on a horse. We were out in the field, Pop and I, checking irrigation ditches. He had dismounted to work on a gate, and I sort of casually walked my horse away until we were out of sight over a hill. My heart was pounding and my stomach tight, but something in me needed to do this. It was time. I jabbed with my heels and gave a *click-click* and my horse took off. Pop never saw—I don't know why I was embarrassed to try it in front of him. But from that day on I was a completely different rider, confident, willing to take off after any steer or descend any ravine.

It was in Boy Scouts I learned to backpack, picked up a bit of first aid know-how, and a few other merit badges. I also learned to use colorful language there. But the real adventures began when I started backpacking on my own, with only a friend or two. One summer I was high in the Sierra Nevada with my friend

Kevin when a tremendous thunderstorm rolled in and brought with it a downpour that lasted for hours. We had pitched our tent in a small glen surrounded by granite, and after an hour or so of playing cards we noticed that the bottom of our tent was beginning to squish and undulate like a water bed. What had happened was that the entire region was one massive field of rock, and the small glens of pine and grass were in fact bathtubs underneath, which began to saturate, then fill with water as the runoff made its way into every low place.

Soon our sleeping bags would be soaked, along with everything else, and concerns about hypothermia kicked in. We were both brand-new Christians, so we prayed, asking God for help. In about five minutes the rain stopped, and we grabbed all our gear and the tent—still fully erected—and carried the whole camp to a higher hill above the runoff. We pitched the tent again, threw our gear inside, and dived in ourselves as the rain started back up. We laughed and thanked God, thought this was how everyone lived the Christian life. Then went back to our poker game.

The next year—I think we were nineteen—we took a road trip across the West. I owned a tan '68 Volkswagen Squareback—my first car, and a young man's first car is a big part of the cowboy stage. It had a Kadron conversion kit that switched the engine from standard (and sluggish) fuel injection to dual overhead carbs, making the Squareback fast, unreasonably fast, and very loud. Fast and loud equal Happiness when you're a young man. You might recall that the engines in the Squarebacks sat in the rear of the wagon, just under a panel, but the overhead carburetors made it impossible to close the panel so mine sounded like a small airplane inside. You had to yell to have a conversation. It also made it very warm in winter and unendurably hot in summer. So we raced down the highways of the West with the windows rolled down and the stereo cranked up.

We ran out of gas somewhere in Wyoming, way up in the mountains, far from any town. I had been so focused on finding a "secret fishing spot" a local had let us in on that I failed to watch the fuel gauge, and when we stopped I looked down to realize that we were running on fumes. I felt like an idiot. It was more than twenty miles back to town. We were both new Christians, so we prayed and asked God to help us. Simple, but heartfelt prayers. I heard God reply, *I will bring you gas*. That was the first time I ever heard the voice of God. With childlike faith I thought, *Great. Let's go fishing*. So we left the car by our campsite and spent a few hours down at the river. When we returned, there was a group of young people in their twenties stopped there, and they said, "We're headed into town this afternoon—is there anything you guys need?" I said, "Yeah, could I catch a ride with you? I need to pick up some gas," to which they replied, "No problem, man, we'll bring it back for you." So we went back to fishing.

"Taking to the road" often plays a big part of the cowboy (or ranger) stage, as you see with the hobbits in *The Fellowship of the Ring*, and with Balian in *Kingdom of Heaven*, and with a group of young men in an old Western favorite of mine, *The Cowboys*.

John Wayne plays his typical crusty old self, in this case a rancher who can't find enough men to help him drive his herd the four hundred miles to market. He is forced to employ boys in their early to midteens, and the story is the coming of age of those boys. They take to the trail together on a high—and dangerous—adventure that calls forth daring and courage, and requires hard work and determination—things a boy-becoming-a-young-man needs to learn in order to face life head-on.

The Power of Experience

There's an old African proverb that goes like this: "I hear, I forget. I see, I remember. I do, I understand." How true this is when it comes to masculine initiation. Men, and boys, learn by *doing*; we learn through experience. This is no doubt true for women as well, but I can vouch that it is essential and irreplaceable for men and boys. It's one thing to be told you have what it takes. It's another thing altogether to *discover* that you do, through some trial brought up in an adventure, or through some test that hard work demands. The experience is both a revelation and a kind of authoring, in that it reveals to you what you are made of and writes the lesson on your heart.

For masculine initiation is not a spectator sport. It is something that must be *entered into*. It is one part instruction and nine parts experience.

This is what lies behind the story of David and Goliath I

mentioned in chapter 1. The armies of Israel have drawn up against the armies of the Philistines, but not a single shot has been fired from any bow. The reason, of course, is Goliath, a mercenary of tremendous size and strength, renowned for his skill in combat. He's killed many men bare-handed, and no one wants to be next. David is barely a teen when he goes to the camp and sees what is going on. He offers to fight the giant, at which point he is brought before the king, who in turn attempts to dissuade the lad. Saul says, "You are not able to go out against this Philistine and fight him; you are only a boy, and he has been a fighting man from his youth" (1 Sam. 17:33 NIV). Sound advice, the likes of which I wager any of us would offer under the same circumstances. David replies:

> Your servant has been keeping his father's sheep. When a lion or a bear came and carried off a sheep from the flock, I went after it, struck it and rescued the sheep from its mouth. When it turned on me, I seized it by its hair, struck it and killed it. Your servant has killed both the lion and the bear; this uncircumcised Philistine will be like one of them, because he has defied the armies of the living God. The LORD who delivered me from the paw of the lion and the paw of the bear will deliver me from the hand of this Philistine. (vv. 34–37 NIV)

Being a shepherd, as I explained earlier, is the cowboy stage, and David learned lessons here that would carry him the rest of his life. The life of the shepherd was not a sweet little life with lambs around. It was a hard job, out in the field, months camping out in the wild on his own. And it had its effect. There is a settled confidence in the boy—he knows he has what it takes. But it is not an arrogance—he knows that God has been with him. He will charge Goliath, and take his best shot, trusting God will do the rest. That "knowing" is what we are after in the cowboy phase, and it only comes through experience. And may I also point out that the experiences David speaks of here were physical in nature, they were dangerous, and they required courage.

HARD WORK

One hot July morning in the summer of 1973 my grandfather drove me out to a field where an old red Massey Ferguson tractor was parked. Attached to the tractor was a large disc plow. He explained that he wanted the field plowed up so that he could plant alfalfa, and showed me how he wanted the rows to lie perpendicular to the terrain to make the best use of the irrigation. Then he said, "I'll see you around suppertime" and drove off. I was stunned. Up till this moment, I had used the tractor only a bit around the barns, doing small jobs. Here he was, entrusting me with a powerful piece of equipment on a whole other level. Standing out there in the field, I felt a little frightened. And profoundly honored. *He thinks I have what it takes.* I was thirteen at the time.

I want to be quick to say that the time of the cowboy is *not* meant to be merely one of unending adventure. Many fatherless young men find life in some adventure like kayaking or snowboarding, and they stay there and make it their world. They adopt the culture of the sport, the language and the clothing that identify them as really cool adventurers. They might take a job at a resort or as a guide, in order to do it 24/7. But the adventure loses its transcendence, and they find themselves stuck in their journey. They are modern-day Peter Pans, refusing to grow up as men. On the surface they seem alive, and free, and daring. Beneath, they are uncertain and ungrounded. And they have broken the hearts of many young women who loved the adventurer, and didn't understand why he wouldn't go on to be the warrior, and the lover, and the king.

The balance here to adventure is that this season in a young man's life is equally a time of learning to work. No doubt David had many adventures in the field, as anyone knows who has spent time outdoors. Adventure has a way of finding you out there. But the context of those months and years was *hard work*. Was Jesus an outdoorsman? We have no record, but we do find him often turning to the wilderness during his ministry years, and it is not a long reach to assume that those walks in the desert and nights on the mountain didn't start, out of the blue, when he took up the ministry. That he turns there for comfort and refreshment and to be with his Father indicates a history of doing so. We do know he worked in the carpenter's shop, and that is more significant than most profiles of Jesus understand. Working with wood and tools, side by side with your father, does things for a young man that few other situations offer.

This is the secret to the simple wisdom of the movie *The Man from Snowy River*, another story of a young man coming of age. Jim, a young man of about seventeen or so, has lived with his father up in the Snowy River backcountry of Australia ever since he was a boy. A beloved son, working alongside his father with wood and tools and horses. When his father is killed in a logging accident, Jim is confronted by the other mountain men who have carved a life out of the wilderness: "You have to earn the right to live up here," they say, making it clear that Jim has to go prove himself before he can simply take over his father's place. It might seem a cruel thing to say to an orphaned young man, but it was true and exactly what the young man needed to hear. It sets Jim on his journey to becoming that man. He hires on as a laborer at a big ranch down in the valley, wins the heart of the girl, proves himself and his integrity when all is in doubt. He becomes the *man* from Snowy River.

There is another old movie, *Captains Courageous*, the story of a Massachusetts halibut fisherman around the turn of the twentieth-century. This story also revolves around a boy's transformation. Harvey Cheyne is a twelve-year-old rich kid, the only son of a widowed tycoon. A spoiled brat, but not a beloved son. His busy father has no time for him. The boy falls off an ocean liner he and his father are taking to Europe, and is rescued by one of the fishermen. At first, the lad is a royal pain in the butt. But he is befriended by the fisherman, becomes his shipmate, and experiences something of the beloved son. He learns to work—something he has never done in his life—and the effect upon him is dramatic.

I had a summer job in a potato packing shed, not far from my grandfather's ranch, when I was fifteen. My grandfather had been a foreman in those sheds when he was a younger man, and my father, my uncle, and my cousins had all done stints there as well, loading the fifty-pound sacks of spuds onto dollies, which they'd roll onto the waiting railcars outside. So it had become a sort of tradition for the young men in our family to do time in the sheds. Of course, my father had married, moved to the city, and it was as a city kid that I came back to work in the sheds of a farm town of about four thousand people. All the other laborers were migrant workers by that time, Hispanics who spoke no English, and we had an absolute ball, our common language being laughter and the practical jokes we'd play when the foreman wasn't looking. It was hard work, and I'd eat like a bear when I got back to the ranch and then hit the hay and sleep till dawn.

This sort of initiation was common to every boy-becoming-a-young-man before the industrial revolution. But you don't have to live on the farm to experience this. Not at all. To this day, my favorite job remains the work I did as a janitor in my church. There were three or four of us on staff, vacuuming floors, cleaning toilets, setting up chairs for the Sunday services. We'd paint, and fix roofs, and do all sorts of odd jobs, again, laughing most of the time, playing practical jokes on the ministers, putting anonymous notes in their mailboxes. Lunchtimes we'd play pickup basketball in the gym, eventually pulling the rest of the staff into the games. I've heard those games are still going on to this day. I loved the simple, hard work, learned so much that I still use today. Except how to fix sprinklers.

Life is hard. While he is the beloved son, a boy is largely shielded from this reality. But a young man needs to know that life is hard, that it won't come to you like Mom used to make it come to you, all soft and warm and to your liking, with icing. It comes to you more the way Dad makes it come to you—with testing, as on a long hike or trying to get an exhaust manifold replaced. Until a man learns to deal with the fact that life is hard, he will spend his days chasing the wrong thing, using all his energies trying to make life comfortable, soft, nice, and that is no way for any man to spend his life.

UNDEVELOPED AND WOUNDED

The cowboy heart is wounded—or at least, undeveloped, but more often wounded—in a young man if he is never allowed to have adventure, and it is wounded if he has no one to take him there. It is wounded if he has no confidence-building experiences with work. And on both counts, it is wounded if the adventure or the work is overwhelming, unfit to the heart of the boy, and if he repeatedly fails there.

I believe I've told the story before of a man I knew whose

mother would not let him, as a boy, ride on a roller coaster. He could see it there, day after day, because they lived across an empty field from the amusement park. But he could never win permission to join his friends in the adventure. That is emasculating, and it applies to those parents who never let their boys ride bikes on a dirt path, forbid them to climb a tree or jump on a trampoline, keep them indoors most of the time. They might say they are only acting out of love and concern for the boy, but the message is, "You'll get hurt. You can't handle it. You don't have what it takes." Often this is the voice of the mother, whose nature is mercy but who must learn to let her son face danger.

For that matter, a boy is wounded when his parents simply let him live in front of the TV, or the computer, or the video games young men love. I have nothing against computers or video games per se (with the added warning that some games are very wicked in their content and ought to be sent to the Abyss). In general they are benign, and boys love them because they work in the same way a boy's brain works, with spatial relationships and all that, but I am *very* concerned when they take the substitute of a *real* adventure.

In his study of the development of male homosexuality, Joseph Nicolosi is especially worried about the boys who are too frightened to go outside and play with the other lads in the neighborhood. He calls them "kitchen window" boys, who stay inside and merely watch. Some boys are more inherently fearful than others; some are made fearful by overprotective parents. Either way, it is a wound to let a boy stay there.

It is emasculating to shelter a young man from everything dangerous. Yes, there are risks involved, and as the young man moves into his mid- to late teens, those bodily risks increase dramatically. I don't let my sons go ninety miles an hour on an ATV, though they would like to. There is wisdom in parenting, but we must accept the fact that there is risk also. You might recall the line from the movie *Seabiscuit*, during the debate of whether to let Red even ride again after his accident, because he might further injure himself. It is another jockey who warns them, "It's better to break a man's leg than it is to break his heart."

On the other hand, I just heard the story of a young man this weekend who worked with his father on a ranch when he was growing up. They spent their summers in the high country, at a cow camp with no running water, and they'd climb in the saddle before dawn and ride until after dark. The father brought no food or water along, and when the boy complained of thirst the father would tell him to "suck on a rock." The boy was ten years old. That is abuse of the first order, putting a boy through paces that would break a grown man.

When it comes to work, the principles are the same. Too little is a wound, as is too much. I've been intentional about letting my sons grow accustomed to and able to handle power tools. I've heard too many stories about the father and son working on a project together—a pinewood derby car or a tree fort—and the father never letting the son use the tools. These boys are now hesitant men. Sure—he can get hurt. That is why it's important. Like my grandfather with the tractor, it says, "I believe in you. You have what it takes." Now, I am not saying I let a six-year-old use a chain saw. But of course you let a young man take risks even in his work.

A young man's heart is wounded when he has no one to take him into the adventures his soul craves, no one to show him how to shoot a free throw or jump his bike or rock climb or use a power tool. This is how most young men experience fatherlessness— there is no man around who cares and who is strong enough to lead him into anything. His father might be physically present, but unavailable in every way, hiding behind a newspaper or spending hours at the computer while the young man waits for the father who never comes. Much of the anger we see in young men comes from this experience, because they are ready and fired up but have no outlet, no place to go. So it comes out in anger.

And a young man's heart is wounded when he repeatedly fails. Of course, failure is a part of learning and every cowboy gets thrown from his horse. But there needs to be someone at his side to *interpret* the failures and setbacks, to urge him to get back on the horse. If you weren't the beloved son, the testing that comes with this stage can feel unkind, cruel, a sort of rejection—especially if you are on your own. My friend Morgan remembers a day in gym class when he was wounded with one of the defining wounds of his life. He was overweight, and when the teacher called him up to do pull-ups, "I just hung there. It was so humiliating. I remember thinking, *I am not a boy, and I will never be a man.*"

The masculine soul needs the trials and adventures and

experiences that bring a young man to the *settled confidence* David showed before Goliath—the lion and the bear experiences. All of these experiences of the cowboy stage are driving at one basic goal: to answer his Question. The boy-becoming-a-young-man has a Question, and the Question is, "Do I have what it takes?" It is a father's job to help him get an answer, a resounding *Yes!* that the boy himself believes because it has come through experience. The father provides initiation by arranging for moments—through hard work and adventure—when the Question is on the line, and in those moments helps the young man hit it right out of the park. The father is to speak into his son's heart deep affirmation. Yes, you do. You have what it takes. He needs a hundred experiences that will help him get there, and he is wounded and emasculated when he is kept from those experiences, or left on his own to interpret them, or when no one is there to help him in his journey toward initiation.

Raising the Cowboy

You have a strength, and it is needed. When a man feels that to be true of him, he rises up and engages like a man. As a boy begins to become a young man, there are some key issues at stake. He needs to know he possesses a genuine strength, and he needs to know that strength is ultimately for others. There is a bravery that must be cultivated in him, for it will be called upon in every other stage of his life. Adventure comes into play to develop the masculine soul, because adventure calls us out, requires us to be something we want to be but aren't sure we are. Adventure nourishes and strengthens a man's heart in ways that cannot be fully articulated, must be experienced. It works like nothing else I know. As Norman Maclean wrote of the men who parachute into rugged country to fight forest fires,

> It is very important to a lot of people to make unmistakably clear to themselves and to the universe that they love the universe but are not intimidated by it and will not be shaken by it, no matter what it has in store. Moreover, they demand something from themselves early in life [the cowboy stage] that can be taken ever after as a demonstration of this abiding feeling. (*Young Men and Fire*)

As I explained in *Wild at Heart*, adventure is a spiritual longing set in the heart of every man. Notice that in the tales told in Scripture, whenever God gets hold of a man he takes that man into an adventure of the first order. Abraham, called out of Ur, to follow this God to a land he has never seen, never to return. Jacob, wrestling with God in the wilderness in the dead of night. Peter, called out of the boat to Christ in a raging storm. Paul, called out of his prominent role as the ultimate Jew, to become apostle to the Gentile world of east Asia. The stories of his journeys are one narrow escape after another.

Teddy Roosevelt's story would be worth reading. His life as a boy was emasculating—overweight, pampered rich, poor eyesight.

His mother even dressed him as a girl when he was young. When he began to come into manhood, he knew he needed to develop *as* a man, knew he needed initiation. He left the refined culture of the upper-class East Coast elite and headed west, bought a ranch in what was then simply called the Dakotas. He began to camp, ride horseback, hunt, not only for the personal pleasure they brought him but for the *effect* they had on his soul. Eventually he became a big-game hunter in Africa, bringing down bull elephants and male lions on the charge, only moments from his own death. Using the example of hunting adventures, Roosevelt explains how he intentionally developed a manly courage and strength:

> In hunting, the finding and killing of the game is after all but a part of the whole. The free, self-reliant, adventurous life . . . the wild surroundings, the grand scenery . . . all these unite to give the career of the wilderness hunter its peculiar charm. The chase is among the best of all national pastimes; it cultivates that vigorous manliness for the lack of which in a nation, as in an individual, the possession of no other qualities can possibly atone.
>
> [The hunter] must, by custom and repeated exercise of self-mastery, get his nerves thoroughly under his control . . . the first two or three bucks I ever saw gave me buck fever badly, but after I gained experience with ordinary game I never had buck fever at all with dangerous game. In my case the overcoming of buck fever was the result of conscious effort and a deliberate determination to overcome it. More happily constituted men never have to make

this determined effort at all—which may perhaps show that the average man can profit more from my experiences than he can from those of the exceptional man.

Let the man who thinks himself "average" take special note—Roosevelt, a man who struggled with his weight, had poor eyesight, and was never initiated by his father, was able to develop that confidence we see in David before Goliath. He went and found initiation, and embraced it. Too many men I know missed the cowboy stage; too many boys are not being guided through it. So we must go back and pick up where *we* left off, intentionally, as Roosevelt did. He went on to become a warrior, by the way, a lover and a good king, in my opinion, and all that was built on this cowboy stage.

Now, I need to clarify something. The place of adventure in a man's journey is very, very important. Unfortunately, we live at a time when adventure has become big business. Magazines are filled with photo essays of the latest gear, the coolest places, the most extreme adventurers—men and women kayaking off waterfalls, kiteboarding, looking for the ultimate big waves. Much of this adventure is not initiation at all; it tends to be merely exotic (often extreme) play, nothing more than adolescent indulgence. The characters that often fill these pages are postmodern Peter Pan types.

Without a *context*, adventure is for the most part . . . just adventure. Nothing wrong with it per se, but I know from experience, and you can hear in an honest interview with professional adventurers, that it is empty. That's partly why they have to keep pushing the limits. It's not enough to climb El Capitan—now you have to do it speed-climbing, alone, in a single day. Crazy stuff like that. In the *Wild at Heart Field Manual* (you ought to read and work through it if you haven't already done so), I explain that there are levels of adventure, from casual to crucial to critical. Casual adventures are mostly what fill the pages of those magazines. I believe they *can* develop a boy and a man for more important adventures, and they can be a key part of initiation *if they have a context*, and *if they are intended to be a first step* toward more important adventures. You don't go from being a couch potato to a strong man in a day. But we mustn't get the idea that masculinity is just one outing after another.

Adventure comes to us in many forms—a flat tire two hundred miles from nowhere, an invitation to join our friends in the woods, a yearning to completely change our careers. As men, we need to seek adventure, and embrace it when it comes unlooked for. *Not* to live a selfish life, not to squander our lives fishing and golfing, not the Peter Pan syndrome, but because there are things that need to be strengthened and called out in our souls as men, and that happens out there, in adventure.

You'll recall how crucial my grandfather's ranch was to my cowboy years. The time was a gift, and like so many gifts, it was eventually stolen. My grandfather developed brain cancer and died rather quickly when I was eighteen. It hurt so intensely I couldn't even bring myself to go to the funeral. My story with horses and ranches ended that year. Fast-forward two and a half decades. Some friends with a ranch here in Colorado invited me to go riding for the day. Oh, how I looked forward to this. Even though it was a cold late-January day, with snow on the ground, I was rarin' to go. But not the horse.

Their riding season had been over for a couple of months, and he wasn't too happy about being sent out alone with a new rider, kept trying to turn back to the barn. A battle began between us, and my heart sank. *C'mon, God. You know how much this means to me. Why does it have to be such a hassle?* The horse was becoming incorrigible and it began to appear to me as a picture of my life. *Why does everything have to be so hard?* (How many of you guys have said that?) I feared that any moment it would turn into a rodeo, so I was about to turn around and give in, surrender. But something in me urged on. As I began to work with a stubborn horse on difficult terrain—we were sliding up and down some steep, snowy trails—a thought began to occur to me. *You are in this, aren't you, Father?*

One of the ways the Question is written on my heart is "Do I have what it takes to be a good horseman?" For another guy, the issue of horses doesn't matter much. The Question finds him elsewhere—at work, or maybe in sports, or finances. But for me, the question was there, with horses. And as I crested out on top of the ridge, horse now under control, difficult terrain conquered behind me, a sort of satisfaction emerged in my heart, quite unlooked for. God wanted to answer the Question, through experience, and only a day like this would have done that for me. As I drove home I wondered, *How much of my life have I been misinterpreting? How many things have I just written off as hassle or "life is hard," or even as warfare, when in fact God was in it, in the difficulty, wanting to Father me?*

Father, take me there. Take me back to things that were lost, or unfinished, or never even started. Take me into the cowboy stage and do this work in my soul. Father me here. Give me eyes to see, both where you have been fathering me and I didn't know it, and where you are initiating me now, though I might be misinterpreting it. I want to be brave and true. I want a strength, and I want to offer it to others. Lead me on.

5 WARRIOR

Gird your sword upon your side,
O mighty one.

—Psalm 45:3 NIV

When Alexander the Great died, his massive
empire was divided among several high-ranking officers in his
cabinet. What we would refer to as the Middle East, including
Israel, came under the rule of the Seleucids, who continued
Alexander's mission to Hellenize the locals, making all the world
Greek in its customs and values. What began as the seemingly
innocent importation of Greek culture became increasingly hos-
tile, and eventually violent. The Seleucid overlords took a special
hatred of the Jewish insistence in worshipping one God, seeing
it—as have so many dictatorships since—as a threat to their
regime. In 165 B.C. a Greek officer holding command over the
village of Modiin—not too far from Jerusalem—ordered the

Jewish villagers to bow to an idol and eat the flesh of a slaughtered pig, acts that struck at the heart of Judaism, at the heart of the people for whom such a command was unthinkable. Blasphemy.

The people refused, an argument ensued, and the Jewish high priest Mattathias killed the officer with a sword. The villagers—led by Mattathias's five sons—took up arms against the rest of the soldiers and killed them as well. Mattathias and a growing number of his followers fled to the hills, from there launching a resistance movement against their Hellenistic oppressors. Meanwhile, Antiochus IV (heir to the Seleucid Empire and a cruel enemy of the Jews) seized control of the temple in Jerusalem, set up in the Holy of Holies a statue of Zeus, and commanded the Jews to worship him. Those who refused to abandon God and his commands—including circumcision—were persecuted, mothers put to the sword with their infants hanging round their necks.

Meanwhile, Mattathias had died, leaving command of his growing forces to his son Judah Maccabee, who led his outnumbered and outarmed troops against a far superior force (ten thousand Jews against more than sixty thousand Greeks and Hellenized Syrians) and eventually routed their enemies from Jerusalem. They cleansed the temple, tore down the desecrated altar (including the idol) and rebuilt one from uncut stones, after which they held a feast of worship and dedication. Of course, I am referring to the origin of the Jewish Festival of Lights, Hanukkah. Historian Thomas Cahill observed that "there are humiliations a proud people—even one oppressed for generations—cannot abide."

Indeed. It may take time, and require repeated provocation, but eventually a man must come to realize that there are certain things in life worth fighting for. Perhaps, when we appreciate the truth of this, we can better understand the heart of God.

A WARRIOR GOD

I don't fully understand the modern church's amnesia-plus-aversion regarding one of the most central qualities of God understood for centuries before us:

The LORD is a warrior; the LORD is his name. (Exod. 15:3 NIV)

The LORD will march out like a mighty man, like a warrior he will stir up his zeal; with a shout he will raise the battle cry and will triumph over his enemies. (Isa. 42:13 NIV)

But the LORD is with me like a mighty warrior; so my persecutors will stumble and not prevail. (Jer. 20:11 NIV) [The NASB translates mighty warrior "dread champion." Goliath was a dread champion; the mighty men of David were dread champions. King James has it as "a mighty terrible one."]

Lift up your heads, O you gates; be lifted up, you ancient doors, that the King of glory may come in. Who is this King of glory? The LORD strong and mighty, the LORD mighty in battle. (Ps. 24:7–8 NIV)

Our God is a warrior, mighty and terrible in battle, and he leads armies. It is *this* God that man is made in the image of. I spoke of this in *Wild at Heart*, but some things bear repeating, because a man will be in a much better place to enter the stage of the warrior if he knows this is thoroughly grounded in Scripture, supported by Scripture, *compelled* by Scripture.

The Philistines went up and camped in Judah, spreading out near Lehi. The men of Judah asked, "Why have you come to fight us?" "We have come to take Samson prisoner," they answered, "to do to him as he did to us." Then three thousand men from Judah went down to the cave in the rock of Etam and said to Samson, "Don't you realize that the Philistines are rulers over us? What have you done to us?" He answered, "I merely did to them what they did to me." They said to him, "We've come to tie you up and hand you over to the Philistines." Samson said, "Swear to me that you won't kill me yourselves." "Agreed," they answered. "We will only tie you up and hand you over to them. We will not kill you." So they bound him with two new ropes and led him up from the rock. As he approached Lehi, the Philistines came toward him shouting. The Spirit of the LORD came upon him in power. The ropes on his arms became like charred flax, and the bindings dropped from his hands. Finding a fresh jawbone of a donkey, he grabbed it and struck down a thousand men. Then Samson said, "With a donkey's jawbone I have made donkeys of them. With a donkey's jawbone I have killed a thousand men." (Judg. 15:9–16 NIV)

A Sunday school story? Perhaps. Though I have never heard the lesson explained, "And this, children, is what happens when the Spirit of God comes upon a man." Yet that is clearly the lesson of the passage. Samson becomes a great and terrible warrior when, and *only* when, the Spirit of God comes upon him. The rest of the time he's just short of an idiot. What does this story tell us about the God whose Spirit this is? And it's not just Samson, my friends. "When the sons of Israel cried to the Lord, the Lord raised up a deliverer for the sons of Israel to deliver them, Othniel. . . . The Spirit of the Lord came upon him," and Othniel went to war (Judg. 3:9–10 NASB). "So the Spirit of the Lord came upon Gideon," and Gideon went to war (Judg. 6:34 NASB). "Now the Spirit of the Lord came upon Jephthah," and he went to war (Judg. 11:29 NASB). "And the Spirit of the Lord came mightily upon David," and one of the first things he did was kill Goliath (1 Sam. 16:13 NASB). I repeat my question: What does that tell us about the God whose Spirit this is?

Our image of Jesus as a man has suffered greatly in the church, but perhaps no more so than our image of Jesus as a warrior. What was it that made Jesus so outraged that he sat down, and in an act of premeditated aggression, built for himself a whip of cords and then, having built it, used it on the merchants occupying the temple courtyards (John 2:13–17)? "Zeal for your house will consume me" (John 2:17 NIV). Is this the kind of behavior you'd expect from the Jesus you were taught of, gentle Jesus meek and mild? Yes, Jesus could be immensely kind. But what is this other side to him we see in the Gospels? "Woe to you, teachers of the law and Pharisees, you hypocrites! You travel over land and sea to win a single convert, and when he becomes one, you make him twice as much a son of hell as you are" (Matt. 23:15 NIV). Oh, my. Them's fightin' words.

THE REASON FOR THE WARRIOR

Our God is a warrior because there are certain things in life worth fighting for, must be fought for. He makes man a warrior in his own image, because he intends for man to join him in that battle.

One day the young man Moses, prince of Egypt, went out to see for himself the oppression of his kinsmen. When he witnessed first-hand an Egyptian taskmaster beating a Hebrew slave, he couldn't bear it, and killed the man. A rash act, for which he becomes a fugitive, but you see something of the warrior emerging in him. Years later, God sends him back to set all his people free, and, I might add, it is one intense fight to win that freedom. David also fights, battle after battle, to win the freedom of his people and unite the tribes of Israel. Something in the man compelled him, that same something that wouldn't allow Lincoln to simply sit by and watch the Union tear itself apart, wouldn't permit Churchill—despite the views of many of his own countrymen—to sit by and let the Nazis take over Europe unopposed. For he knew that in the end they would have England, too.

There are certain things worth fighting for. A marriage, for example, or the institution of marriage as a whole. Children, whether they are yours or not. Friendships will have to be fought for, as you've discovered by now, and churches, too, which seem bent on destroying themselves if they are not first destroyed by the enemy who hates them. Many people feel that earth itself is worth fighting for. Doctors fight for the lives of their patients, and teachers for the hearts and futures of their students. Take anything good, true, or beautiful upon this earth and ask yourself, "Can this be protected without a fight?"

You see this in the movie *Cinderella Man*, based on the true story of boxer James J. Braddock. He loses his reason to fight, and thus he begins to lose his fights. But when the Great Depression hits, and threatens to tear his family apart, a fire is lit in the man. He makes a startling comeback, felling contenders much younger and stronger than he. His manager, stunned, says, "Where did that come from?" It came from within, from a sleeping warrior awakened. In a press conference he is asked a similar question, "What are you fighting for?" "Milk," he says. The survival of his family. Sometimes the battle has to strike close to home in order to rouse the warrior in a man. Perhaps that is why God often allows it to strike so close to home.

So in the movie *The Cowboys*, those young wranglers who hit the trail still wet behind the ears become warriors at the end of the story. Their boss is gunned down by outlaws, shot in the back, unarmed, their cattle stolen, and it rouses them to the next stage of their masculine maturity. They arm themselves and go after the villains, killing most of them and rescuing the herd. So, too, when Simba finally comes out of his Peter Pan stage, living the easy life out in the jungle, his first act as a young man is to fight his uncle for the kingdom. Evil typically doesn't yield its hold willingly. It must be forced to surrender, or be destroyed. Balian is trained to be a warrior by his father, and his first act upon reaching the Holy Land is to lead a charge of cavalry against the enemy. But one of my all-time favorite stories comes at the end of The Lord of the Rings.

The beloved sons are toughened as cowboys, and they go on to become warriors in their own right. After helping Aragorn their king win the last great battle for Middle Earth, the hobbits make their way home. Then comes one of my favorite chapters in all the books: "The Scouring of the Shire" (totally overlooked in the movie). For when the hobbits finally return at the end of their quest (and initiation), they find their beloved Shire in the hands of the evil one. The trees are cut down, the rivers polluted, their people enslaved, the charming inns shut down or replaced by jails. The wolf is not merely at the door. He has made himself at home. They will not stand for it.

This was too much for Pippin. His thoughts went back to the Field of Cormallen, and here was a squint-eyed rascal calling the Ring-bearer "little cock-a-whoop." He cast back his cloak, flashed out his sword, and the silver and sable of Gondor gleamed on him as he rode forward. "I am a messenger of the king," he said. "You are speaking to the king's friend, and one of the most renowned in all the West. You are a ruffian and a fool. Down on your knees in the road and ask pardon, or I will set this troll's bane in you!" The sword glinted in the westering sun. Merry and Sam drew their swords also and rode up to support Pippin . . . the ruffians gave back. Scaring Breeland peasants and bullying bewildered hobbits had been their work. Fearless hobbits with bright swords and grim faces were a great surprise. And there was a note in the voices of these newcomers that they had not heard before. It chilled them with fear.

The beloved sons had returned as warriors. And a good thing for the Shire, too, and its gentle inhabitants.

PASSIVITY

One of the saddest of all the sad stories in the history of the people of God comes shortly after the dramatic exodus from Egypt, as they stand on the brink of a whole new life in the land God had promised:

But you were unwilling to go up; you rebelled against the command of the LORD your God. You grumbled in your tents and said, "The LORD hates us; so he brought us out of Egypt to deliver us into the hands of the Amorites to destroy us. Where can we go? Our brothers have made us lose heart. They say, 'The people are stronger and taller than we are; the cities are large, with walls up to the sky. We even saw the Anakites there.'" Then I said to you, "Do not be terrified; do not be afraid of them. The LORD your God, who is going before you, will fight for you [Not "comfort you." Not "be with you in your distress, defeated by your enemies." *Fight for you*], as he did for you in Egypt, before your very eyes, and in the desert. There you saw how the LORD your God carried you, as a father carries his son, all the way you went until you reached this place." In spite of this, you did not trust in the LORD your God. . . . Then you replied, "We have sinned against the LORD. We will go up and fight, as the LORD our God commanded us." (Deut. 1:26–32, 41 NIV)

But it was too late. Their decision *not* to fight is what led to their wandering in the wilderness for forty years. We often cite that part of the story, talking about our own wilderness experiences, embracing the wilderness saga as if it were inevitable. No, that is not the lesson at all. We have forgotten *it was avoidable.* The reason they took the lamentable detour into the wilderness was because they would not fight. To be more precise, the wilderness was a punishment, the consequence of refusing to trust God, and fight.

Remember *The Two Towers*, and the reluctance of Théoden king of Rohan to fight? "I will not risk open war." I shake my head. What is it in human nature that just won't face the reality of war? Why, my son heard it again just the other day, in his Bible class of all places. "We are not supposed to resist Satan. That's God's job." That is dangerous thinking, and unbiblical.

> Resist the devil. (James 4:7 NIV)
>
> Resist him. (1 Pet. 5:9 NIV)

We live in a world at war. We are supposed to fight back. It is apparently a difficult reality to embrace, as witnessed by the passivity that marks much of modern Christianity. We just want the Christian life to be all about the sweet love of Jesus. But that is not what's going on here. You may not like the situation, but that only makes it unattractive—it does not make it untrue.

AGGRESSION

I said that Israel's refusal to fight in order to claim the Promised Land is, to me, one of the saddest stories in the Bible. But it is not the saddest. When it comes to the record of men in particular, our worst moment has to be Adam's failure and the introduction of original sin, which got us into this whole mess in the first place. It was a failure marked by *passivity*. Eve was deceived, says Paul, but not Adam (1 Tim. 2:14). He sinned for other reasons, unspecified, but when we look at the story we have some evidence to go by. Adam doesn't engage, doesn't intervene, doesn't do a thing. He is created to act, endowed with the image of a mighty God who acts and intervenes dramatically. Adam did not, and whatever else got passed on to us men from the first man, we know that *paralysis*—another word for *passivity*—is certainly one of them.

Years ago I had a chance to do a great good for a ministry I was working for. The manager over my division was doing a lot of damage to his staff; several people had quit, and finally he wanted to know why. He was headed to my office to ask me what I thought was going on, and I ducked out, pretended to be on my way to a meeting. I wimped out, dodged conflict. I hate that about me. What is this in me that just doesn't want to engage when Stasi is having a hard day? Why would I rather work on the car, or on this book, than enter into the dark waters of relationship? Why do I hesitate when one of my boys wants to tell me, through tears, about how hard things are at school? You know of what I speak.

There are regions of a man's world that he allows to become a sort of DMZ, an "I won't bother you if you don't bother me" land of capitulation and passivity. It might be the family finances, or a struggle with in-laws. It might be a growing conflict in his church, or community. We look for the path of least resistance, and that is rarely the right path to take. I'm saddened to think of all the things I've just surrendered over the years, given up without a fight. It is essential that a man overcome this inherent passivity, this paralysis we got from Adam that lies deep in our bones. To be men we must, with the help of God, overcome it intentionally, repeatedly, on front after front across the seasons of our lives.

There is a scene in the Western *Open Range* that captures this beautifully. Typical of Westerns and their mythic simplicity, the town has been overtaken by bad guys, as John says the world lies under the power of the evil one (1 John 5:19). The crooks have installed their own sheriff, and hired gunslingers to frighten the citizens into submission. Two cowboys come to town to get some justice for the murder of their comrade, and the near murder of a boy they have befriended. In the saloon, they try to rouse the men of the town to action. One of the local tradesmen says, "It's a shame what this town's come to," to which one of the cowboys replies, "You could do something about it." "What?" the frightened man replies. "We're freighters. Ralph here's a shopkeeper." Then my favorite line: "You're men, ain't ya?"

The assumption is that whatever else a man might be, he ought to be a fighter. I noticed this assumption in the rosters of the tribes of Israel as they came out of Egypt. The families and clans are arranged and numbered as fighting men (Num. 1:3). And remember—these are not trained soldiers, but runaway slaves. I doubt any of them had held a weapon in his life, yet it is assumed that if he's a man, he's a fighting man. Given who and what he is, Scripture assumes that a man acts, a man intervenes. Passivity has no place in the lexicon of true masculinity. None. And to overcome passivity, God has set his warrior heart in every man.

THE HEART OF A WARRIOR

When I was twenty-one, I wanted to change the world. That's not an uncommon passion for a young man, as witnessed by the many revolutions and reform movements led by young men. Bob Woodward and Carl Bernstein were in their twenties when they broke the Watergate scandal. It was young college students in their twenties who took a stand in Tiananmen Square against the Communist overlords of China. Luther entered seminary in his early twenties, and he was thirty-three or thirty-four when he nailed his theses to the door at Wittenberg, in the prime of his warrior years. Wilberforce was twenty-one when he entered Parliament, and twenty-eight when he took up his battle against the British slave trade. It's safe to say that most of Jesus' disciples were young men, as that was the tradition in the rabbi-pupil relationship, and they, too, were passionate about changing the world, ready to call fire down from heaven to make it happen (Luke 9:54).

I was a young Christian when I entered a secular college, and zealous, which equaled a good amount of grief for any professor taking what I held to be a condescending view of Christianity. I had a philosophy class I enjoyed very much, and hardly a day went by that my hand didn't shoot up during a lecture, to challenge the assumptions of the agnostic and, thankfully, gracious professor. For me, the Truth was worth fighting for. Many young men have felt that way. You hear it in the music of nearly every generation, the cry for a better world, "the songs of angry men," the musical *Les Misérables* had it, "the music of a people who will not be slaves again."

About that time I started a theater company in L.A., and we were out to change the world. We worked late hours, threw ourselves into it with zeal. We took to the streets in the summer of '84 to perform evangelistic street dramas when the crowds came to Southern California for the Olympics. It was bold, and daring, just the sort of enterprise a young warrior throws himself into. During those years there were a numbers of wildfires that swept across the Los Angeles foothills, fueled by the Santa Ana winds blowing off the desert. I helped a neighborhood evacuate, stayed behind to man a water hose in order to soak down the roof of the home of an elderly woman we knew who couldn't defend her home herself. Something in me felt so alive, and brave, facing danger to make a difference.

As I explained in *Wild at Heart*, the warrior is hardwired into every man. This is true because he is made in the image of God, who is the Great Warrior. Like Father, like son. It is also true because it constitutes a great part of man's mission here on earth—to join the Great Warrior in his battle against evil. It is this aggressive nature that will enable us to overcome the passivity and paralysis we inherited from Adam. In fact, we are siding with one or the other—the warrior or the paralyzed man—in every decision we make, every day. Encouraging the warrior as it begins to come into full force in a young man's life will be a great help to him as the years unfold, for you and I know how hard the battle is if we've spent years in passivity.

I am not saying every man must join the military, though that is a noble calling; there are many ways for the warrior to emerge. Over the ages the pen has proved mightier than the sword, as the old saying goes. What I am saying is that there is an inherent

aggressiveness written in the masculine soul. So it shouldn't surprise us—though many parents are still a bit unnerved—when
you see the warrior emerge in the boy when he is very young. As
for the *stage* of the warrior, I believe it begins in the late teens—
about the time we send a young man to war. When God tells
Moses to arrange the fleeing slaves into tribes, he has them "number by their divisions all the men in Israel twenty years old or
more who are able to serve in the army" (Num. 1:3 NIV). So here
it is marked at age twenty, and that seems confirmed in so many
revolutions fueled by young men.

The heart of the warrior says, "I will not let evil have its way.
There are some things that cannot be endured. I've got to do something. There is freedom to be had." The heart of the warrior says, "I
will put myself on the line for you." That is why it must come before
the lover stage, for he will need to do that time and time again in his
marriage, and it is passivity that has broken the heart of many
women. The warrior nature is fierce, and brave, ready to confront
evil, ready to go into battle. This is the time for a young man to stop
saying, "Why is life so hard?" He takes the hardness as the call to
fight, to rise up, take it on. He learns to "set his face like a flint," as
Jesus had to do to fulfill his life's great mission (Isa. 50:7).

UNYIELDING

Let's take a story from early in the ministry of Jesus—the trial in
the wilderness—to see what we might learn of the warrior. It is

one of the first stories told about Jesus, and I think it's important to point out that the focused record of his life (the same is true of David) takes up with his warrior stage, which ought to tell us something about how vital this stage is. The story takes place in the wilderness. First, we are told that Jesus has fasted for forty days. Stop right there—it is the warrior in a man that enables him to do that. How much hardship a man will endure, how long and tenaciously he will persevere is determined by the amount of warrior within him. A young man may have a job he hates, under an arrogant boss, but if he sees it as warrior training, he will endure. A man in a difficult marriage can persevere only if he finds the warrior inside.

The time of the warrior is the time of learning discipline, a concentration of body, mind, and spirit. Of course, all our military boot camps are saturated with discipline, because they know that when all hell breaks loose on the battlefield, a man has to have something to fall back on other than emotion. Spirits are high before you actually meet the enemy, but in the chaos of warfare high spirits can vanish in an instant. This is true far beyond the sands of Iwo Jima, and especially true in spiritual warfare. I was stunned to read about the discipline practiced by one of the early Desert Fathers, Saint Antony, considered the founder of Christian monasticism:

> He practiced the discipline with intensity, realizing that although his foe had not been powerful enough to beguile him with bodily

pleasure, he would surely attempt to trap him by some other method, for the demon is a lover of sin.... [Antony's] watchfulness was such that he often passed a night without sleep ... he ate once daily, after sunset, but there were times when he received food every second and even every fourth day. His food was bread and salt, and for drinking he took only water ... regularly he lay on the bare ground. (Athanasius, *The Life of Antony*)

It's the warrior that enabled the young man in his twenties to do that, for he had found his cause and his king. Now, there is discipline and there is discipline. The church has largely presented discipline as "kill your heart and just do the right thing." That is terrible. It wearies the soul, and ends up destroying the heart—the very faculty you will need in the face of great trial and testing. Good discipline *harnesses* the passions, rather than killing them. When Jesus "set his face like flint" toward Jerusalem, he manifested an inner resolve that came *from* deep within, from his heart. He would not be deterred from his mission. A young man will need this strength of heart, whether to finish his PhD, or to hold fast his convictions under persecution, or to master an art form—all of which take great discipline, fueled by passion.

This inner resolve is what is so sorely tested in Jesus as Satan comes to him in the wilderness, probing his defenses, looking for some angle, some hook to get Christ to give in and yield to temptation. He does not. This is absolutely essential to the warrior, to develop an unyielding heart. This is where *we* will be most profoundly tested. Though he is stoned, whipped, thrown into prison for preaching the gospel, Paul is undaunted. He will not be turned, and for that we have the books of Ephesians, Philippians, Colossians, and Philemon. Bunyan wrote *Pilgrim's Progress* from prison, and Alexander Solzhenitsyn continued his resistance of Soviet Communism from the gulag. I will not yield, I will not be a quitter—that is the warrior coming out.

> If you can keep your head when all about you
> Are losing theirs and blaming it on you,
> If you can trust yourself when all men doubt you
> But make allowance for their doubting too,
> . . . Or being lied about, don't deal in lies,
> Or being hated, don't give way to hating,
>
> If you can bear to hear the truth you've spoken
> Twisted by knaves to make a trap for fools,
> Or watch the things you gave your life to, broken,
> And stoop and build 'em up with worn-out tools:
> If you can force your heart and nerve and sinew
> To serve your turn long after they are gone,
> And so hold on when there is nothing in you
> Except the Will which says to them: "Hold on!"
> Yours is the Earth and everything that's in it,
> And—which is more—you'll be a Man, my son!
> (Rudyard Kipling, "If")

The warrior must learn to yield his heart to nothing. Not to kill his heart for fear of falling into temptation, but to protect his heart for nobler things, to keep the integrity of his heart as a great reservoir of passionate strength and holy desire. That was Jesus' battle in the wilderness, as Satan tried this way and that to get him to surrender his integrity. *You don't need to trust God to meet your needs—make these stones become bread. Prove God cares for you—throw yourself off this building. You don't need to go the way of the cross—worship me and I'll give you the kingdoms of this world.* Jesus will not give in. This is no easy thing to do, as the history of man attests. As your own history attests.

And notice—at the end of the battle, "angels came and ministered to Him" (Matt. 4:11 NKJV). I never paid much attention to that; it almost seems an afterthought. But there is something for us to see here, or it would not have been included in the record. Jesus needs some ministering to, which gives us the sense that he was sorely taxed by the event. I take some comfort from this, both because it is a reminder of the human side of the incarnation mystery—Jesus really was a man—and because that sure has been my experience of these battles. When they are over, I am utterly drained and need some ministering myself.

By the way—there *is* a place for comfort in the masculine journey, a place for mercy and rest and being ministered to. It's not all trial and test and battle, not by any means. It's just that most often, good comfort comes *after* the fight, and is so much more enjoyable in this way. One of the spoils of war.

WOUNDED

The heart of the warrior is wounded in a boy and in a young man when he is told that aggression is flat-out wrong, unchristian, that niceness equals godliness. He is wounded when his attempts to rise up as a warrior are mocked, or crushed. He is wounded when he has no one to train him, no king to give his allegiance to and no cause to fight for.

A colleague of mine in a ministry years ago had a little boy, their firstborn, and he wrote an article about how the little guy wanted to knock down his block towers but the father would not let him. "Life is not about tearing down, but about building one another up." Good grief, what classic religious nonsense. Does not the Scripture say, "There is a time for everything . . . a time to tear down and a time to build . . . a time for war and a time for peace" (Eccl. 3:1, 3, 8 NIV)? Little guys want to know they are powerful. In the ethics that a three-year-old understands, knocking his block towers over is simply basic power. Wow. Look at me. I'm strong. Telling him that is sinful is emasculating, as is never letting him play with weapons, never play battle or superhero. I'm sure he'll grow up to be a very nice man.

The heart of the warrior is wounded in a young man when he attempts to be a warrior and is shamed. I remember a day from the seventh grade, during PE class, when I saw a friend of mine being bullied by a bigger kid at the drinking fountain. My friend was overweight, and already having a hard time in gym class, and this bully was mocking him, laughing at him, forcing him to drink and then kicking him so that he would get water all over himself. I could see my friend was scared, and ashamed. And this bully was such an arrogant, self-important little poser I had to intervene. The coaches were nowhere to be found, so I ran over and told him to "knock it off—leave him alone." The bully turned around and knocked out two of my teeth. Just like that. Now I was the one who felt weak and ashamed.

Never winning at anything, getting bullied, pushed around, outright beat up has crushed many a young warrior's heart, sent him into passivity. "I'll never try that again." I needed a man there to tell me that I was brave, that I did the noble thing, that though we don't win every fight there are still things worth fighting for. And to show me how.

The wound is doubled when the beating comes from his own father, or perhaps an older brother. For that matter, the warrior is wounded when a boy has to become a fighter too soon, as is the case when his father tells him, "Don't be such a crybaby" and sends him back out to face a pack of boys who are bullying him, or when he lives in a volatile home where the shouting and anger make it clear that it's every man for himself. Or when he doesn't get to win at anything. My sons love to wrestle, but they would soon lose heart if I flipped them over and pinned them every time.

On the other hand, if the father is passive, how will the young man learn to be a warrior? Nothing rouses anger, frustration, and mounting disrespect in the heart of a boy as does his father's passivity. The young men in the movie *The Patriot* don't understand why their father won't fight, and one of them is killed when he tries to rescue his brother because his father won't. (Many boys and young men take on family battles because their father won't.) When he does finally rise up, the boys discover that their father is a great warrior, and they respect him utterly. A man I knew, a pastor of the "sweet love of Jesus" school, told me one day that his son had up and joined the marines. The man was bewildered. "I don't know why he did this." I'll tell you why—because you never taught him to be a warrior, so he went to find someone who would.

Finally, the heart of the warrior is wounded, or abandoned, or sometimes let loose in very bad ways, when the young man does not have a king and a cause to serve. Bryan, a colleague of mine, told me a few weeks ago, "I've been meeting with a group of guys from my church for a while now. A question keeps coming up: 'What do we do without a king?' The men I am around are deeply frustrated. They called themselves 'Ronin,' samurai warriors without a master. My simple swing at an answer is that God is the Master in every stage. He is the Father when we are beloved sons, and he is our King when we are warriors. I saw in these men that the longing for a king runs deep and that this simple answer was not satisfying." I understand their frustration. For years I was angry at older men who would not act like kings. It cuts deep into our fatherlessness.

But there is hope. Jesus no longer had Joseph around when

he entered his warrior stage. On a human level, he was fatherless. But we know he was *not* alone. We, too, have a Father who
is a great warrior, and he will raise us as warriors, if we'll let
him, if we will embrace the initiation that comes with this stage.
There is a warrior in you, by the way. However it has been
handled up to this point in your life, it can be restored, recovered, and made strong. The promise of Scripture is that the
Father is raising us to be sons just like Jesus, meaning, you shall
be as valiant as he was.

> Father, show me where I have lost heart as a warrior. What did I
> miss here? What was wounded, and what was surrendered? Take
> me back to those times and places when the warrior in me was
> shut down. Awaken and restore the warrior heart in me. Train me.
> Show me what I have surrendered, where I am walking in passivity.
> Teach me to have an unyielding heart. Rouse me. I am willing. I
> am yours.

RAISING THE WARRIOR

How does God raise the warrior in a man?

As I think back over the past twenty years, I see now that
nearly everything I've learned as a warrior, I've learned on the
field of battle, in the school of reality, the classroom of my life. I
began to see the answer to the question: "How does God raise the
warrior in a man?"

Hardship.

Something in you knows it's true. I think this is where we have most misinterpreted what God is up to in our lives. As long as we are committed to the path of least resistance, to making our lives comfortable, trial and tribulation will feel unkind. But, if we are looking for a dojo in which to train as a warrior, well then—this is the real deal. What better means than hardship? What better way to train a warrior than by putting a man in situation after situation where he must fight?

I was on an overseas trip a few months ago, scouting the readiness of a country for a mission we had in mind. As I drove with my colleagues to the airport, we asked Jesus for any advance words he might have for us (a very wise thing to do before going into battle). *Give way to nothing.* I had no idea what was about to happen, but in retrospect I understand why he said *to nothing*, rather than to certain things in particular, because it felt like I was hit with everything but the kitchen sink. Our hosts were good men, but driven, neither cowboys nor warriors, in many ways still trying to implement the business model to Christianity. The enemy whispers, *You know more than they do*, and the pull to make a subtle, arrogant agreement set in, which would have ruined our relationship. *Dismiss them*, he says. *No*, I reply. *No arrogance.* Five minutes later it turned to, *They are dismissing you.*

We walked into a hotel and the receptionist looked up. "May I help you?" She was the mirror image of a girl I dated in high school, before I'd become a Christian. The enemy was there in a moment, using an old wound to try to usher in seduction. *Remember? You can have that again.* First pride and now lust—how many men have fallen here? "No, thank you," I said to her. "We're just here for a meeting." One of our colleagues ended up failing to meet us there. Judgment gives it a try: *What a jerk.* Resentment steps in: *He's always failing you.* My father wound was abandonment, and the enemy knows that, and tries to make me feel as though my friend— and everyone else—has abandoned me. I won't go with that, and then it's worry and self-reproach: *Maybe something's wrong. Maybe you said something that hurt him.*

Someone makes a comment about the difficulty of putting on the conferences we'd planned there, and fear rushes in. *What if this doesn't work? There's no guarantee, you know. This isn't going to work.* I fight off fear. Ten minutes later it's not failure, but success. *You could make a lot of money off this, you know.* It was true, we could, but that was not why we'd come. "Let's cut the rate we're charging," I said, "Let more guys in." The team looked a little puzzled, and self-doubt is there: *You idiot. You shouldn't have said that.* I swear to you, this all took place in the first hour and a half after landing. We had three more days to go.

In the hotel room that night, I dream of the girl in high school, wake in the dark, disoriented, in some other country in the middle of the night in a sweat, and have to pray for an hour to get back to sleep. Resignation, which so often accompanies weariness, followed. *This isn't worth it.* "Yes, it is," I say aloud in my room at 3:00 a.m. More prayer. The following morning, I am irritated at our hosts, who locked the keys in the rental car. *Idiots. Dismiss them. Get irritated at them.* This went on and on, nonstop, for days. The waitress is beautiful, and seduction tries again. I refuse, and then comes, *The reason you don't want her is because you're gay.* Okay, now they've even thrown in the kitchen sink. Thank God I've seen enough fights to recognize it for what it was, and I hung on, giving way to nothing. It felt like hanging on to a branch over a cliff. Praying constantly—in the elevator, the car, the bathroom—being gracious to people who continued to make mistakes, fighting all this internally.

I could tell you a hundred stories like that. From a single year.

You *will* be tested. Like Jesus' desert trial, the enemy comes, probing the perimeter. He knows your story, knows where the weak spots are. But this *is* our training. This is the spiritual equivalent of, "Take a high guard, like this. Strike from high. Like this. Do it. Blade straighter. Leg back. Bend your knees. Sword straighter. Defend yourself." This is how we develop a resolute heart. We make no agreements with whatever the temptation or accusation is. We repent the moment we do stumble, repent quickly, so that we don't get hammered. We pray for strength from the Spirit of God in us. We directly—and this is the one thing so many men fail to do—we *directly* resist the enemy, out loud, as Jesus did in the desert. We quote Scripture against him. We command him to flee.

By the time it's over, you'll wish a few angels would drop in and minister to you as well. I pray they do.

Be Intentional

Life will provide a thousand sessions for the raising of the warrior. Turn your radar on during the day, and intentionally *don't* take the path of least resistance. Take the road less traveled. If you are the kind of man who just hates any sort of conflict, then walk into some. When an awkward subject comes up at work—or at home—don't run. Move toward it. Ask hard questions. Hold your ground. The phone rings, and you can tell by the caller ID it's someone you don't want to talk to. Pick it up. Engage. That's the key word—*engage*. I come home tired, and just want to veg. Luke needs help with his homework, Stasi wants to talk, Sam and Blaine have something they need. I choose to engage, and my tiredness fades a little as the warrior wakes up.

There are things we can do intentionally to develop the warrior. Sports can do this. It's amazing what a little pickup game of basketball can bring out in a man. Competition is good, and ought to be a part of every man's life. Adventure also provides many settings for the warrior to come forth. Several years ago my family and I were staying at a cabin in the mountains for a long weekend when some really foul weather moved in. While Stasi and the boys stayed inside by the fire, sipping cocoa with marshmallows, I strapped on my snowshoes and headed out for a high mountain lake. It was about seventeen degrees outside, with a windchill of minus five. Cold enough to freeze the water in my Nalgene. No one else was on the trail. I chose to go *because* the weather was awful, *because* I would be the only one out there. I wanted to be tested, to endure hardship and suffering. Something in my soul craved it. At that time in my life I spent most of my days in a cubicle, and I felt I was going soft inside. So, as I said in the cowboy stage, head into something that will really test you, and you'll see the warrior emerge.

Be decisive. Every time a man makes a hard decision, the warrior in him is strengthened. Notice those places you are normally passive, and do the opposite. What are you surrendering these days? Go take it back. Warrior stories would do you good, too. Study David's life as a warrior. Read other stories of the great warriors of Scripture. Watch the movies that stir the warrior in you. (Bring your sons into this.) Read true accounts of warrior heroes, like *We Were Soldiers Once . . . and Young*, *D-Day*, and *Citizen Soldiers*.

FACING YOUR ENEMY

Eventually we find that we must face our enemy head-on. Now we come to direct conflict with foul spirits and the kingdom of darkness. I know many men who have avoided this far too long. Good men, for the most part, but intimidated from any direct conflicts with the enemy, and preferring to stay in the human realm. "I'm a reluctant warrior," a friend confessed this week. "I'd rather stay in the—what was it—the Shire." But he was made a king this year over a company, and he has been forced to fight spiritual warfare "like never before. It's been intense." Which reminds us that a king had better be a warrior first, or else he will fold under the assault, or lead his people into passivity, like Théoden.

We have the example of Jesus in the wilderness as a model for how we must resist Satan (and all foul spirits—for Satan has many subordinate demons working for him). Jesus treats him like a real person (not a human being, but a fallen angel with an intellect and personality). He doesn't treat the temptations and accusations and assault simply as if they are weaknesses within himself; nor does he act as though they will go away if he tries to ignore him. He directly confronts the demon present out loud, with authority, and with Scripture. Later, in the book of Acts, we are given a similar example through the life of Paul:

> Once when we were going to the place of prayer, we were met by a slave girl who had a spirit [a demon] by which she predicted the future. She earned a great deal of money for her owners by fortune-telling. This girl followed Paul and the rest of us, shouting, "These men are servants of the Most High God, who are telling you the way to be saved." She kept this up for many days. Finally Paul became so troubled that he turned around and said to the spirit, "In the name of Jesus Christ I command you to come out of her!" At that moment the spirit left her. (Acts 16:16–18 NIV)

Paul commands the demon to leave, out loud, and firmly, "in the name of Jesus Christ." Meaning, by the authority of Jesus Christ. That is how it's done. Jesus triumphed over all foul spirits through his cross (Col. 2:13–15). All authority in heaven *and on this earth* is his now (Matt. 28:18). He gives us his authority to overcome foul spirits (Luke 10:19; Eph. 1:18–21). That is why Paul commands the demon "in Jesus' name."

This will become more and more necessary as you rise up as a warrior, and take back ground that you have surrendered, and begin to advance the kingdom of God. Direct confrontation, modeled for us by Jesus, and Paul. (You'll want to read up on this. Ed Murphy's *The Handbook of Spiritual Warfare* is excellent, as is *Victory Over the Darkness* and *The Bondage Breaker* by Neil Anderson, and *Spiritual Warfare* by Timothy Warner.)

The simple rule for identifying foul spirits is, "What is it doing? What is its effect?" Is it fear you suddenly feel? Then you're dealing with a spirit of fear. Is it overwhelming discouragement? Then you've probably been attacked by a spirit of discouragement. Jesus models for us in the wilderness trial that first, we make no agreements with it. Give no room in your heart to it. Then, send it away in his name. Your life is the training ground, and when it comes to spiritual warfare, it's all live-ammo training. Take it seriously.

Some Counsel from the Battlefield

One Battle at a Time

The enemy's first plan is to keep a man out of the battle altogether—through fear, or self-doubt, through bad theology or ignorance, through his wounds, or through the passivity we inherited from Adam. If that doesn't work (and it's worked with many a man), and a man rises up to be a warrior, the enemy switches to dog pile. Bury you in battles. What he'll do is try to lure you into battles that aren't yours to fight. Be careful here—you don't want to take on every battle that comes your way. Hitler swore he'd learned from WWI that he would never again let Germany fight a two-front war. He ended up doing it himself, and that's a big reason why he lost the beaches of Normandy—his troops were tied up in Russia. Thank God they were. But don't let yourself be lured into battles that aren't yours to fight, no matter how urgent they might seem.

After my partner Brent died, there was great need for me to take over as the hub of his counseling practice. So many people were in need. But as I prayed about it, seeking God's counsel, what I sensed Jesus asking me was, *If you didn't need to prove you were a good man, would you do this?* (God often answers our questions with another question.) I didn't need to think long about my answer. *No*, I said, *I wouldn't.* Then he said, *You have no need to prove it, John.* Released from any need to come through in that situation, I didn't take on that battle, and became a writer instead. Ask Jesus, *Do you want me to fight this?* Get your orders from your King.

Fight Your Battles Once

You don't want to get worn out through hours of speculation, working over and over in your mind how some event is going to go. You don't know how it's going to go, and I have never once found speculation helpful. It simply ties you in knots. Resist it. Don't fight your battles twice—once in worry and anticipation, and the second time when you actually enter into the event itself. Cross that bridge when you come to it, as the saying goes. This will require strength and resolve, resisting speculation, and it will strengthen the warrior in you. It's another way of learning not to yield your heart—in this case, to worry and fretting.

During Any Important Event, Assume It's Warfare

In normal day-to-day living, hassles, accidents, setbacks might simply be that and nothing more. A flat tire is a flat tire. But during an important event, Stasi and I, and the fellowship we live in, have found it's nearly always warfare. Treat it as such. And by "important event," I mean anything redemptive—a mission, of course, but also a source of joy, like an anniversary. The enemy is out to steal your joy more than anything else.

Resist It Quickly

Don't let things get a foothold. However tired you may be, however distracted or inconvenient the moment, *now* is the time to fight. "Ye must be watchful," says à Kempis, "especially in the beginning of the temptation; for the enemy is then more easily overcome, if he is not suffered to enter the door of our hearts, but is resisted at the first knock." Don't kid yourself, saying, "I'll deal with this later." I'm stunned how I will actually welcome a distraction, an opportunity *not* to deal with it. I'll check my e-mail, or take a phone call, or go wander through the house, check the pantry for something to eat *in the very moment I should be praying.* That's passivity and surrender in subtle form. When you pray, or resist, or act decisively *in the moments you least want to,* the warrior in you is strengthened. Next time you'll be even stronger.

You Won't Feel Like a Warrior

This is important to know, for we long to feel brave and powerful in battle. But that is rarely the case. In the *midst* of battle, you will often feel confused, disoriented, perhaps overwhelmed, troubled with self-doubt. You will certainly feel the spirits that are present, and they will try to make you believe it's *you* that is angry, or prideful, or whatever assaults you. Set your face like a flint. It will clear, eventually, and you will again feel the presence of God and who you truly are. In the midst of it, war is chaos.

Stay with It

It takes more than a single skirmish to win a battle, and a hate-filled enemy usually will not yield at a single swing from us. Keep at it. The enemy is testing your resolve. Show him that no matter how long it takes, you fully intend to win.

It Will Make You Holy

The enemy is coming, Jesus told his disciples, but "he has no hold on me" (John 14:30 NIV). I love that, I just love it. Jesus is so clean, they've got nothing on him. It tells us something vital about warfare. First, that holiness is your best weapon. Spiritual warfare will make you holy. Trust me. Why is the enemy using that particular angle on you at this particular moment? Invite Christ in. Is it an occasion for repentance? Deeper healing? Strengthening feeble places? Good, that's good. You'll be a better man for it. The battle we find ourselves in gives a whole new purpose to holiness. The call is not to "be a moral man because it's decent." The call is to "become a holy man and a warrior, for you are needed in this battle, and if you do not become that man, you will be taken out."

The recovery of the warrior is absolutely crucial to the recovery of a man. All else rests on this, for you will have to fight, my brothers, for everything you desire and everything you hold dear in this world. Despite what you feel, or what you may have been told, you have a warrior's heart, because you bear the image of God. And he will train you to become a great warrior, if you'll let him.

Father, you are a great Warrior, and I am made in your image. I am your son, and a warrior, too. Open my eyes to see how you have been developing the warrior in me. Show me where I've misinterpreted what has been happening in my life. Give me the strength and resolve to rise up and accept my warrior training. And when I am losing heart, give me your grace and encouragement to hang in there, all the way through to victory. In Jesus' name.

6 LOVER

I found the one my heart loves.

—SONG OF SONGS 3:4 NIV

TO SAY THAT I HAD COME TO THE MOUNTAINS, ALONE, to be with God, would sound as though I'd come of my own accord, making the journey seem noble, austere, gallant. But that would not be honest. I came to the mountains because I was *summoned*. Exhausted from months of battle and hard labor, I needed to get away, knew that I needed to get away, yet somehow could not bring myself to do it. You know how that is—you find yourself on the treadmill, hating it, but accustomed, even addicted to it, and getting off seems like an inconvenience, even if it will save your life. Thank God, something deeper in me was being called— a longing that is hard to describe, a compelling ache for Beauty. That is how God drew me.

The great danger for the warrior is not defeat, but success. As

I said before, what the evil one does to a good warrior—if he cannot take him out, cannot keep him from entering the battle at all—is to bury him. Dog pile. Make it all about battle. Make it constant. One battle after another, like Jeremiah Johnson faces as his fame becomes known, like David faces because of Saul's jealousy and then because his enemies learn he is the man to contend with. Easy Company of the 506th in WWII kept getting one tough assignment after another because they could handle them. Like Jesus, who has to duck out of town because word has gotten out and everyone has come to the door with some need or another (Mark 1:29–37).

We must not let the battle become everything.

So for several years I had made a practice of withdrawing to some remote place to be with God, usually for three days. Up till now my mode had been to backpack into wilderness in order to assure solitude and all that it brings. But this year I was just too tired to hike up any mountain like a pack mule with my camp upon my back. So I chose a place I could drive to, up a long four-wheel-drive road, hoping that would place me high enough in the mountains to be where my heart comes alive, which for me is above the tree line in the very high country. When I finally pulled over and parked, I was in a broad mountain meadow surrounded by glacial peaks, wildflowers in full bloom, the sun so hot because there was so little atmosphere left up there to filter it.

I forsook my usual ritual of first setting up camp, took my fly rod and walked out to the middle of the meadow, stood there for a moment, gave a deep sigh, and let it all go, all that I had left behind, in order to allow all this beauty some room to come in. The warmth, the smell of meadow grasses and wild mint, the sound of the little stream, the peaks all round—I stood there for some time to let the encompassing beauty enfold me. Then I began to fish.

The stream there runs about five to seven feet wide, making its way through the meadow rather whimsically, with twists and turns only nature can explain, in no apparent hurry to be any- where. The brook trout that live in that stream are tiny, about six inches long, and despite a brief summer followed by long, harsh winters spent under snow and ice, they are vibrant and energetic. Delicate little creatures with green backs wormed crisscross with patterns the color of moss, red fins rimmed with white, and doz- ens of lavender spots along their sides within which lies a bright pink dot. As Hopkins says, "Glory be to God for dappled things / for skies of couple-color as a brinded cow / for rose-moles all in stipple upon trout that swim." I caught a few, and held them in the glacial waters, amazed at their beauty and life, then returned them to make it through another winter. "Little poems" is what I called them. Living flashes of beauty.

Having lost a fly in the bushes—I wasn't casting well, partly because it had been a long time since last I fished, but mostly because I was distracted by so much beauty—I knelt down to tie on another, found myself kneeling in shallow water that rippled over a shelf of stones and pebbles on the inside of a bend in the creek. The water here was flowing only three inches deep—just enough to wet the stones into fullness of color, as you'll notice how a stone will leap to life when you wet it, as even the streets look their best after a rain. The pebbles beneath me spread out in a mosaic made of a thousand granite stones, most of them between the size of a quarter and a dime. Purples, browns of many hues from tan to chocolate, yellows, black, white, ground to utter smoothness by the glaciers, laid out like a Byzantine mosaic. Each stone was dappled, being granite, and together they made a dappled pattern, which was in turn dappled by the rippling waters rippling sunlight over them. I could have gazed at the fluttering mosaic all afternoon. It was captivating, and soothing, and intriguing—all the things that gentle, intimate, flowing beauty offers.

I was still kneeling in the shallow water, and as I looked down, my eye fell upon one small stone in particular, as if it were somehow illuminated, which is not quite right because it was one of the darker stones in the mosaic, almost black, so it could not have stood out for its brightness. But those of you who have had this experience will know what I mean, when in a crowd of people one face stands out to you almost to say *Look at me*, or when you are reading a passage and one sentence causes you to stop and linger while all the rest of the page fades into the background but for that phrase. The stone was in the shape of a heart.

A kiss from God. A love note. I was being romanced.

THE AESTHETIC CONVERSION

Now we come to a fork in the road in the masculine journey, a stage that is both essential and, sadly, often overlooked and bypassed by many a man. The stage of the lover. By this I do not primarily mean that time in a young man's life when he falls in love with a girl. Though that is part of it, I don't believe it is the core of the stage or even its ultimate expression. I do hope that there will be a girl in the picture, and that she turns his world upside down. Eve is God's glorious intrusion into the world of cowboys and warriors, for nothing, absolutely nothing, disrupts like Eve, and she is meant to change their lives forever. However, there are movements in the young man's soul that would be best to take place *before* Eve steps into the picture, movements that often do take place but go unrecognized until she is there.

Down through its history the church has held up the good, the true, and the beautiful as a sort of trinity of virtues. As we think over the stages of the masculine journey, we find that the boy begins to understand Good as he learns right from wrong, and the warrior fights for what is True, but when a man comes to see that the Beautiful is the best of the three, then is the lover awakened. As with the other stages, you'll find expressions of it in his youth, but something happens about the same time a young man begins to become a warrior, late in the cowboy stage, late in his teens and into his twenties. Awakening with his passion for a battle you will often find another longing emerging, a longing for

. . . he knows not what. An ache, often expressed in music, or perhaps poetry, a film or a book that stirs him like never before. His soul is undergoing a sort of second birth.

He begins to *notice*. Sees moonlight on water for the very first time. Is stopped by certain movements in a song he loves. Pauses to realize that a snowflake or a flower is really altogether amazing. Discovers authors that stir him with some special quality in their writings. Now yes, it is often aroused by a woman. Buechner tells of a time when as a boy he fell in love with a girl in Bermuda, "and of all the beauty I longed for beyond the beauty I longed for in her." Woman is the personification of Beauty, and it often takes her to turn the young man's attention from adventure and battle, "turn his head," as the phrase has it, and his heart comes along for the turning too. A young writer who came to see me said that he began to write poetry, and lots of it, when first he fell in love. Over time the woman faded from view—it was a high school romance— but the writing continued, his heart awakened. This is the story of the pilgrimage of Anodos in MacDonald's *Phantastes*, where a man is awakened by a particular beauty, from whence he must take a perilous journey to find that it is Beauty itself he longs for.

But often the awakening comes in the world of Nature, especially if the young man has been allowed a generous season in the cowboy stage. You see this in the poetry of David, whose lines are filled with the sun and stars, the dew of the fields, the brooks from which he drank so deeply. Harrington, the driven correspondent, finds more than rabbits in the fields of Kentucky. He learns to see:

If you had known me a long time ago, you wouldn't believe I was in this woods right now, happily listening to *tick-ticking* blackbirds, studying the selaginella mosses. . . . I still can't believe it myself. . . . Every time I come into the old Collins wood, I see something for the first time. The edge saplings, which a decade ago all looked the same to me, are actually a collection of ash, elm, dogwood and hickory. In a hard winter, if you look closely, you'll see that some of their trunks have been girdled near the ground by rabbits eating the soft, nutritious bark.

[Farther off he sees] a wide field that the sun is revealing in shades of sand to ginger to bronze to henna and, a good half-mile away, gunmetal gray that demarcates the tree line along Scaggs Creek from a silver horizon that becomes a stunning delft-blue sky. (*The Everlasting Stream*)

Walking in the woods and fields has awakened the lover, as it has done for many men. The great warrior-king Xerxes, is stopped in his march across Persia, his army of two million stopped behind him, by a sycamore. Stopped in his tracks by a figure of beauty that so captured him he had a replica cast upon gold so that he might remember it the rest of his life. This is very good for the warrior, to be arrested by Beauty. It provides a great balance to his soul, lest he simply be a fighter. The Celts had a phrase, "Never give a sword to a man who can't dance," by which they meant if he is not *also* becoming a poet, be careful how much warrior you allow a man to be.

There was a time, years ago now, when Brent and I were fishing together on the San Juan River in New Mexico. It was September, and the cottonwoods were turning gold and the grasses in the fields were gold as well, and rust and umber, and a deep plum. The heat of the day had lingered long and the sun seemed to hang high in the sky, but now had given way, finally, to dusk, and the cool of the evening. Red-winged blackbirds were trilling in the reeds along the banks of the river. The trout, which had lain all day out of the reach of the sun—and our aims—in the deep black pools, were moving now into the riffles and shallows to rise. A warm breeze was blowing downriver, mixing with the cool evening air rising from the reeds. Time was leaving with the heat of the day, and eternity was taking over the evening.

I looked to the east, and there a full moon was on the rise above the desert mesas, silver and round, poised above the cliffs like the grand dame of the evening on her balcony. And as I looked, a breeze caressed my face, and I knew it was God. A flock of wood ducks flew across the moon, silhouetted by its light, and now all time was gone, and there was only Beauty, and Life, and Friendship. My heart was awakened, wooed by the great Lover.

It is often beyond our reach to describe to others the effect upon the soul that the fellowship of men upon a river, rod in hand, brings. More difficult still to capture the poetry, the beauty that sneaks upon us like the kiss of an evening breeze gently touching your face. But these moments are among the most trea-sured of memories, and they retain the power even still to lift my soul to Beauty, and eternity, to God. Catching a fish doesn't matter anymore, nor does the elk, nor the pheasant in the field, but only what they brought us here to find. As Thoreau said, most fishermen spend their entire lives without knowing it is not fish they are after.

I could tell you of an evening on the Lamar River in the northeastern corner of Yellowstone, also in the fall, also in the evening, when I stood alone in the vast wildness to hear the wolves begin to howl. Or a time late in spring, in the desert canyons of Moab, sitting high on the shelf of a cliff, belaying climbers below me, when the Romance settled in once more. The white sandstone bluffs across the river—looking like great waves frozen in time—were now turning a shade of pink in the setting sun, and the muddy river had become a mirror of those pink bluffs, and the soft blue sky, and the green willows along the bank, swirling the colors as oil swirls upon the water, flowing like a river of paint. The exotic perfume of blooming Russian olive trees was carried by warm breezes down the canyon, and time again disappeared and for a moment all was as it was meant to be.

THE POETIC AWAKENING

We've heard ad infinitum that men are rational beings, along with the supporting evidence that our brains work differently than do women's, and this is true. Spatial abstractions, logic, analysis— men tend to excel in these because we are more left- than right-brained, and the commissural fibers that connect the two hemispheres appear in women in ratios far higher than in men. Women have an interstate uniting both sides of their brains. Men have a game trail. Thus men tend to compartmentalize, a capacity that allows men to handle the atrocities of war, and administrate justice. It also makes them excellent chess players and auto mechanics.

And yet . . .

I don't buy it. Too many men hide behind reason and logic. A man must grow beyond mere reason, or he will be stunted as a man, certainly as a lover. No woman wants to be analyzed, and many marriages fail because the man insists on treating her as a problem to be solved, rather than a mystery to be known and loved. David was a cunning tactician as a warrior, but he was also a poet of the first order. Jesus could hold his own in any theological debate, but he is also an artist (the Creator of this world of Beauty) and a poet (by whose Spirit David wrote the Psalms) and a storyteller. When he says, "Consider the lilies of the field," he does not mean analyze them, but rather, *behold* them, take them in, let their beauty speak, for "Solomon in all his glory was not dressed as beautifully as they are" (Matt. 6:29 NLT). He appeals to their beauty to show us the love of God.

The lover is awakened when a man comes to see that the poetic is far truer than the propositional and the analytical, and whatever physiology might say, I've seen it happen in many men.

I came to Christ not because I was looking for a religion, but because I was looking for the Truth, and, having found it, I knew it must be true across the realms of human culture. I yearned for an intellectually defensible case for Christianity, and I found it first in Schaeffer and then in the Reformed writers, to whom I remain very grateful. There are reasons to believe. My head was satisfied, but my heart yearned for something more. While I found logic in my theology (and went to war against my philosophy professor), I was being wooed by Beauty in the mountains and deserts, in literature and music. Why did they bring me closer to God than analysis? Why did the dissection of systematic theology cut all life out of the living Word? Then I discovered writers like Oswald Chambers, C. S. Lewis, and his sage, George MacDonald. Smart men, all of them, quite capable of making a good argument. But that is not the essence of their glory. They speak to the mind, but also to the heart. More so to the heart.

I began to fish late into the evening, and well after dark, for reasons hard to explain. I hungered for transcendence, for mystery. I began to paint, and the gap between my heart's awakening and the arid propositions of so many self-assured rationalists no longer spoke to me. The riddle was solved when I learned that Chambers had first been an art student before he became a theologian. His biographer David McCasland wrote, "If there was a childhood trait that foreshadowed his gift and passion as a young man, it appeared in the realm of art." Ah, yes, that would explain it. Here is a man who knows the Way of the Heart because he knows and loves Beauty. Long before he went to the mission field (as a mature warrior), Chambers wrote poetry, even a poem in defense of poetry, comparing "those divine essences we call Music, Poetry, Art, through which God breathes His Spirit of peace into the soul" with "mechanical monotony of so-called fact."

I found Lewis's secret in his autobiography:

As I stood beside a flowering currant bush on a summer day there suddenly arose in me without warning, and as if from a depth not of years but of centuries, the memory of that earlier morning in the Old House when my brother had brought his toy garden into the nursery. It is difficult to find words strong enough for the sensation which came over me; Milton's "enormous bliss" of Eden (giving the full, ancient meaning to "enormous") comes somewhere near it. It was a sensation, of course, of desire; but desire for what?

. . . The second glimpse came through Squirrel Nutkin; through it only, though I loved all the Beatrix Potter books. But the rest of them were merely entertaining; it administered the shock, it was a trouble. It troubled me with what I can only describe as the Idea of Autumn. It sounds fantastic to say that one can be enamored of a season, but that is something like what happened, and, as before, the experience was one of intense desire.

. . . The third glimpse came through poetry. I had become

fond of Longfellow's Saga of King Olaf: fond of it in a casual, shallow way for its story and its vigorous rhythms. But then, and quite different from such pleasures, and like a voice from far more distant regions, there came a moment when I idly turned the pages of the book and found the unrhymed translation of Tegner's Drapa and read:

> I heard a voice that cried
> Balder the beautiful
> Is dead, is dead

I knew nothing about Balder, but instantly I was uplifted into huge regions of northern sky, I desired with almost sickening intensity something never to be described.

Lewis goes on to say, "The reader who finds these three episodes of no interest need read this book [*Surprised by Joy*] no further, for in a sense the central story of my life is about nothing else." Nothing else, for what could be greater than the intense desire, the piercing joy of Beauty? He is describing the aesthetic conversion and it led him to God. Through his writings, and the others, through the fields and forests, the art and music, my heart was being wooed in so many ways. For that which draws us to the heart of God is that which often first lifts our own hearts above the mundane, awakens longing and desire. And it is that life, my brothers, the life of your *heart*, that God is most keenly after.

GOD AS LOVER

John Wesley was thirty-five when he experienced the now famous "warming" of his heart—not his mind—toward Christ, and knew in that moment he had become not merely a Christian, but something more—a lover of God. Shortly after, he penned the hymn "Jesus, Lover of My Soul," whose first verse goes like this: "Jesus, Lover of my soul / Let me to thy bosom fly." Down through the years the hymn has left many a hymnologist reaching for a more palatable translation, "the difficulty," as John Julian said, "is the term *Lover* as applied to our Lord." Revisions now in hymnbooks read, "Jesus, Savior of my soul" or, "Jesus, Refuge of my soul," which are touching but nothing close to what Wesley meant. He meant *Lover*.

You'll notice how dominant the "reason and knowledge are everything" approach has been by noticing that men who have fallen in love with God are often referred to in the church as "mystics," a term that gives a sort of honor while at the same time effecting a dismissal. *Mystic*, meaning "inexplicable," which devolves into "unreasonable." *Mystic*, meaning also "exceptional," as opposed to perfectly normal. Odd, even. Difficult to analyze. This from Jaroslav Pelikan would be a classic example:

> The case for the legitimacy of calling Jesus "Lover of my soul" or "Bridegroom of the Soul" stands or falls with the legitimacy, both psychological and religious, of the total mystical enterprise, and

then with the assessment of the particular subspecies of it usually labeled "Christ-mysticism." By a working definition, mysticism may be identified as "the immediate experience of oneness with Ultimate Reality."

I wonder how these men make love to their wives. "My help-meet, would you like to participate in a working definition of oneness at 10:30 p.m. tonight?"

David would have had no problem at all understanding this. The poetry that flowed from the heart of this passionate lover is filled with unapologetic emotion toward God. He speaks of drinking from God's "river of delights," how his lover has filled his heart "with greater joy" than all the wealth other men have found, and he writes in many of his love songs how his heart sings to God. He cries through the night, aches to be with God, for he has found, really found, his life in God: "You have made known to me the path of life; you will fill me with joy in your presence" to such a degree that his heart and soul "pant for you, O God. My soul thirsts for God," his body even longing for God. These are not the words of a dry theologian or moralist. These are not the words of even your average pastor. For him, God's love "is better than life." David is captivated by the Beauty he finds in God. On and on it goes. The man is undone. He is as smitten as any lover might be, only—can we begin to accept this? do we even have a category for it?—his lover is God (Pss. 36:8; 4:7; 6:6; 16:11; 42:1; 63:1; 63:3).

It might be helpful to remember David is a grown man here,

not a teenager, and he is also a battle-hardened warrior with years of hand-to-hand combat experience. What do we make of it, really? If a friend of yours in his forties told you he was losing sleep over a lover, crying all the time, writing poetry and love songs, wasting away until he could be with her again, wouldn't you feel that he'd lost all perspective; that yes, love is wonderful, but c'mon, buddy—pull it together. You'd privately hold the conviction that he was a disaster. And we might also wish we could experience the same.

Humility urges us to take a posture toward David's love affair with God that goes something like this: I have no idea what he's talking about, but he's a far better man than I, and he's found something I need to know, need more desperately than I am probably even aware.

The lover is not as rare as we might think. It's just that when this stage begins to unfold he is not sure how to speak of it, or even whom to tell. Bryan, a colleague, has recently had his world turned upside down. Long has he lived in the realms of "love for God means service for God," and, as an intelligent man, his career most recently has been within the computer industry. Then came the Romancer:

Something has changed. The world is not quite as it seemed. It began with small things. A longer, deeper sigh when I looked at the mountains. Stopping the car on the side of the road to watch the sun set. Seeking beauty at an art festival in Santa Fe. After some weeks, I began to hear him whisper, "I am here. . . . Have you seen me? . . . Do you want to see more?" Slowly, I was taken off guard. My heart began to rest. My eyes were opening to the mysteries and beauty of God. I began to realize that he cared for my heart. God was pursuing me . . . wooing me. My pursuit of beauty had turned around on me. It had become God's pursuit of *me*. I then realized what I was seeing and it broke me to tears. God was acting as if he was *in love* with me.

A friend of mine named Lisa bought an ornate dagger which she named "Beauty," because nothing pierces the soul like beauty. This was a foreshadowing of God's plans for me. He intended beauty to cut me deeply. Through conversations in the presence of this graceful woman, in the presence of a holy, beautiful, and righteous God, he took my heart to every struggle I've ever had to find love in Eve. I was overwhelmed. God spoke to a heartbroken adolescent boy that love was not lost those many years ago . . . love was not to be found in Lisa tonight . . . and it was not to be found when I had worked hard enough to have a great marriage. I saw the beauty and glory of deep abiding in him. Every place I had sought love, every place I had found it, have all been him. His heart for me is greater than I ever knew and I am learning to lean into that. My heart rests more now than it used to. . . . It knows that not everything is a fight. . . . Much of life is simply a romance.

A lover has been awakened by the Great Romancer. At this stage a man's relationship with God opens a new frontier. While in other realms God will remain Father, and Initiator, when the lover begins to emerge God invites the man to become his "intimate one." This is the crucial stage. The danger for the warrior is that life becomes defined by battle, and that is not good for the soul nor is it true to our story, for there is something deeper than battle and that, my friends, is Romance. As Chesterton reminded us, "Romance is the deepest thing in life." Ours is a love story. Anything short of it is a Christianity of dry bones. So Chambers encouraged us, "Get into the habit of saying, 'Speak, Lord,' and life will become a romance . . . one great romance, a glorious opportunity for seeing marvelous things all the time."

FALLING IN LOVE

Having said all this, we can now speak of falling in love with a woman. We *must*. For God has said a man's life is not good without her (Gen. 2:18), so no matter how bold an adventurer or brave a warrior, the man is not living as a man should live unless he makes room for a woman in his life. And, in most cases at this stage, it usually is a woman who comes to awaken the heart of a man.

Now, often what he first sees is not a woman in particular, though he may be looking at her. What he sees is Woman, Beauty itself, tenderness and intimacy and allure, and that is what he falls in love with. We are, all of us, haunted by some memory of Eve. I still remember a beautiful young girl who used to walk home from school past my friend Danny's house, in the sixth grade, and we worshipped her, waited each day for her passing though we never even knew her name. She haunted us, stopped our games of touch football and left us with an ache we also could not name. It is a beginning. The hobbits in their journey are enraptured by Beauty they could never possess—Frodo awakened by Arwen, and Sam by Galadriel.

But, hopefully, the young man will come to know an actual woman, not the universal but the particular woman across the aisle in chemistry class, or walking her dog in the park. They might begin as friends, and then suddenly one day he sees *her*. He notices. For the stage of the lover involves seeing as only those in love can see. That was the beginning of my romance with Stasi. We were classmates and "pals" in high school, and then one summer day a year out of high school I awakened to the Beauty that she was, saw her truly for the first time, and fell in love. Everything changed, not just between us, but in my entire world. I found myself loving many things because I wanted to share them with her—special places, or songs, or artwork I wanted her to see because I knew she would see what I saw in them, and our romance made me love them more, and in sharing them love her more.

The awakening of his heart is essential if a man would truly love a woman. Look at things from her point of view. What does she long for in a man? Every little girl dreams of the day her prince will come. Look at the movies women love—the hero is a *romancer*. He pursues her, wins her heart, takes her into a great adventure and love story. And notice—what is the great sorrow of every woman in a disappointing marriage? Isn't it that he no longer pursues, no longer romances her? Life has been reduced to function and problem solving. What she longs for is what you are meant to become.

So when it comes to loving a woman, the great divide lies between men as lovers and men as consumers. Does he seek her out, long for her, because really he yearns for her to meet some need in his life—a need for validation (she makes him feel like a man), or mercy, or simply sexual gratification? That man is a Consumer, as my friend Craig calls him. The lover, on the other hand, wants to fight for *her*—he wants to protect her, make her life better, wants to fill her heart in every way he can. It is no chore for him to bring flowers, or music, spend hours talking together. Having his own heart awakened, he wants to know and love and free her heart. The sexual difference between lover and consumer is revealing—read Song of Songs and ask yourself, "Does this sound like our bedroom?" The lover wants to "make love" to her. The consumer—well, there are any number of crass phrases men use to talk about getting into bed with her.

Of course the stage of the lover brings with it great pain and suffering, because we are speaking of the heart, and the heart, as we all know, is vulnerable like nothing else. Resilient, thank God, but vulnerable. The heights of joy this stage ushers in are greater than any other, but with them comes the potential for sorrow as deep as the heights are high. That is why he must also be a warrior, and that is why he must find his greatest love in God.

WOUNDED

The heart of the lover never gets to awaken or develop in a man so long as he rejects the heart, chooses to remain in the world of analysis, dissection, and "reason is everything." The lover is wounded in a man (often starting in his youth) when he looks to the woman for that primary love and validation his father was meant to bestow. It is often wounded deeply through the breakup of a young love affair. And it is wounded when he has a sexual encounter far too soon.

There are many reasons a man shies away from the world of the heart and from his own heart. It might be that he is shamed when he tries to go there by a father who thinks that art, creativity, and beauty "are girl's stuff." Thus, to him, the heart is a source of pain and embarrassment. He thinks a man cannot be a true man and live from the heart. It may be that he has simply never been invited to know his own heart.

But we must remember Adam's fall, and the fierce commitment fallen men all share: never be in a position where you don't know what to do. Reason and analysis are predictable, manageable. They make us feel that things are under our control. I believe that is why many men stay there. It's safe—even if it kills your soul.

The lover might come partially alive when a man meets a woman and falls in love, and for a time his heart seems alive and their romance blossoms. But things begin to fade, and neither he nor she knows why. The reason is that he stopped the progression, never went on to know God as Lover. No woman can satisfy this longing in a man's heart, and no good woman wants to try. When he makes her the center of his universe, it feels romantic for a while, but then the planets start to collide. It's not a big enough romance. He will find his heart awakening again when he opens his heart to God, and though he might have to journey there for a season, he'll find he has something to offer his woman again.

As for the search for validation from the woman, how many of you can relate to that? I noticed years ago that when I was speaking before an audience—something I've been doing for much of my career in one form or another—I would often find the most beautiful woman in the crowd and watch her reactions, wanting badly to impress her. It was more compulsive than intentional, but it felt adulterous. And it was. I was looking to her to validate me, merely one expression in a long and fruitless search. My father left me with a huge question mark plastered on my chest— *Am I a man? Do I have what it takes?* Like so many men, I took that question to the woman, and it sabotaged the lover's heart in me. How can you freely and strongly offer love when you are desperate and frightened in a search to get love? Even now, at the stage they ought to act like kings, many men are frightened by their wives because she feels like the verdict on them, and at the same time the Beauty on the screen seems so enticing because she makes him feel like a man.

As I looked back over the relationships I had with girlfriends since high school, I noticed a pattern that troubled me—I always waited until *she* pursued me. Knowing now that is not how a man should act, I wondered, *Where did that begin?* God took me back to my first love, a girl I fell absolutely head over heels for in middle school. I gave her my heart, and she broke it. The first cut is the deepest, as the song so truly says. And after that, I played it safe. Truth be told, I am playing it safe even still, and that has brought Stasi a great deal of hurt and confusion.

Finally, there are those of us who had sexual experiences before our wedding nights, and I've never met a man for whom the fruit of that was good. You'll recall in *Antwone Fisher* that the young sailor is accused of being gay because he won't sleep around, as the other men do. The reason he fears to be with a woman is because he was sexually abused by one as a boy. It brings a terrible ambiguity into the heart of the lover. So does early sexual experimentation. For years I was a cautious lover toward Stasi, and it hurt her. Even on our wedding night she wondered, *Why doesn't he want me passionately?* It introduced a great deal of struggle that took years to heal. The caution had its roots. My first sexual experience was with a girl in high school, and she kept saying, "This will ruin everything." Things did not go well, and what does a young lover's heart learn from that?

Many men who would come alive as a lover feel stuck, their hearts pinned down long ago through some heartbreak. So it would be good to pray:

> Father, God, awaken the lover in me. Stir my heart. Romance me. Take me back into the story of love in my life, and show me where I lost heart. Show me where I have chosen safety over and against coming alive. Show me where deep repentance needs to take place. Heal the lover heart in me. Awaken me.

RAISING THE LOVER

As I explained earlier, the lover emerges around the time of the warrior, those stages overlapping, and let me add he continues right through to the end of a man's life, for the king must be a lover as he must be a warrior, and the sage is a lover long after he has handed the fighting of battles over to younger men. So what we are cultivating here is something that will grow all your life. We are opening a door that must never be shut. And again, before we talk of loving a woman, let us first turn to the romance with God.

How has he been wooing you? What has stirred your heart over the years? The story I told of the mosaic in the stream and the heart rock—God has been bringing hearts to me for a long, long time. It's one of our intimacies. He gave me a rock in the shape of a heart again yesterday, as a reminder. And as I was praying early this morning, I looked out my window and the cloud before me was in the shape of a heart. God has many such gifts for you, *particular* to you, and now that you have this stage of the lover to watch for, eyes to look for the Romance, you'll begin to see them too.

We cannot control what the Romancer is up to, but there is a *posture* we can take. There is an openness to this stage that will enable us to recognize and receive the wooing. So let me ask—are you willing to let go of your insistence to control, meaning, to allow for a life that exists beyond the realm of analysis, to let some portions of your life be impractical, to cease evaluating all things based on their utility and function? Coming closer to the heart, are you willing to let passion rise in you, though undoubtedly it may unnerve you? To permit the healing of some of your deepest wounds? To let yourself be run through as with a rapier by Beauty itself? Are you willing, at some level, to be undone?

Then we may proceed.

To enter into the Romance we must slow down, or we will miss the wooing. Turn off the news and put on some music. Take a walk. Take up painting, or writing or reading poetry. Better still, what was it that stirred *your* heart over the years? *Go and get it back.*

This is hard to do, especially for men who are out conquering the world. But remember—what the evil one does to a good warrior if he cannot keep him in the battle is to bury him with battles. Wear him down with fight after fight. But life is *not* all about the battle. The Romance is always central. Listen again to David:

> Though an army besiege me,
>
> > my heart will not fear;
>
> though war break out against me,
>
> > even then will I be confident.
>
> One thing I ask of the LORD,
>
> > this is what I seek:
>
> that I may dwell in the house of the LORD
>
> > all the days of my life,
>
> to gaze upon the beauty of the LORD. (Ps. 27:3–4 NIV)

He knows battle, knows what it is to have God come through for him. He does not fear it; he is confident as a seasoned warrior is confident. But, he does not make it his heart's desire. What he *seeks* is not battle—what he seeks is the romance with God. "To gaze upon the beauty of the LORD." I've been enjoying some worship songs lately that help me make the shift—"Beauty of the Lord" by Jared Anderson, and "Beautiful One" by Tim Hughs. For we must remember: the battle is for the Romance. What we fight for is the freedom and healing that allow us to have the intimacy with God we were created to enjoy. To drink from his river of delights.

My friend David was asking me the other day about finding the beauty of God. "I think I see God as about 99 percent masculine," he said. "And I think it's hurt me. I mean, I don't find mercy there, or tenderness. Or beauty." He's lived a driven life, as so many of us have. Now he is feeling the emptiness. If a man does not find his life in God, he will become a very thirsty man, and thirsty men have been known to do some very stupid things. Remember Buechner's realization about the girl in Bermuda: "All the beauty I longed for beyond the beauty I longed for in her." Oh, how we must understand this, that there is a Beauty we long for calling to us *through* the beauty of the woman we are enchanted by. She is not the Beauty itself, only a messenger. If we never look beyond, we will try in vain to find it in her, causing both ourselves and the woman a great deal of pain.

But to find it in God, to begin to experience in God what he sent Eve to foretell—now that is what David meant when he said, "Your love is better than life" (Ps. 63:3 NIV).

HEALING THE LOVER'S HEART

The past fifteen years have been a story of healing, repentance, sanctifying and strengthening the lover heart in me. I wanted to be strong for Stasi, to initiate without fear, to have my whole heart to give to her. Yet I felt—how to describe it—uncertain with her, hesitant at times, even fearful at others. On an emotional level, I began to realize there were parts of my heart I had lost or left behind when girls I had loved broke up with me, and I needed to go get my heart back. Last spring I was on a ministry trip when it all surfaced again, and I felt so vulnerable to the beautiful women around me. Not for sex, mind you, but some broken place in my heart was crying out for medication.

God will do this. He will actually bring a woman across your path who speaks to your longings, and your wounds, your fears even, in order to raise the issue *so that he might heal*. This can't be done in the abstract. It must involve those very places in our hearts and souls that have been wounded, or surrendered. It feels dangerous, and it is, but the surgery is needed, and until a man gets that healed he will be more and more vulnerable to a fall. So God will do what he needs to do in order to bring our hearts to the surface. The woman at the hotel—looking just like a young girl I loved in high school—he'll do that, to get to the buried lover.

Now I know—beauty is dangerous stuff. Especially *The* Beauty. As Dostoyevsky warned, "Beauty is mysterious as well as terrible. God and the devil are fighting there, and the battlefield is the heart of man." He may have meant man*kind*, but you and I well know the battle over beauty is terrible in the heart of a *man*. It goes without saying that there is something in the soul of a man that makes him profoundly vulnerable to the Beauty. Every man knows this, knows the breathtaking allure of a woman's form. I'll be flipping through some adventure magazine and whoa—there is a beauty and she stirs something in my heart. Vulnerable doesn't quite describe it. Powerless draws us a bit nearer the condition.

Over the ages men have handled this in basically one of two ways—surrender, or discipline. Surrender can be subtle, as when we let her in, when we allow ourselves to entertain the Beauty even though she is not ours. The lingering glance, the opening of our hearts to her. It can be blatant, as when we masturbate to a photo or a film, or give in to an affair. The damage is terrible, and many good men therefore choose discipline. Force yourself to look away, busy yourself with other things, fight it tooth and nail. Which is *certainly* better than surrender. Joseph ran for his life from Potiphar's wife, and it was the right decision. But discipline without healing doesn't work real well over time, and it can do great damage to our hearts, which begin to feel like the enemy so we'll do what we can to kill them in order to avert disaster.

There is another way. The way of holiness and healing, and it involves what we do *in that very moment*, when our hearts are stirred by a Beauty. God and the devil were doing battle over my heart on that trip I just mentioned, and this is what I wrote in my journal:

> O merciful God, come to me in this place, this very place in my heart. I give this to you. I choose you over Eve. I choose your love and friendship and beauty. I give my aching and longing and vulnerable heart to you. Come, and heal me here. Sanctify me. Make me whole and holy in this very place.

I prayed it over and over, day and night. Whole, and holy. That is what we need. When it comes to emotional entanglements, it might be good to ask yourself, "What girlfriends broke my heart?" And, "What have I done with that?" I spent some time journaling over this, looking back—I even went and found Stasi's middle school yearbook (we went to the same junior high), to see again what Debbie had written there, see her face in order to access that part of my heart, and in that moment, standing in the basement, invited Christ in to bring healing. Some of you men are still in an emotional tie with a woman you knew years ago. You must let her go—along with any photos, letters, mementos you are hanging on to. For some of you, a counselor might be helpful here. But you do not let her go with cynicism or resignation. You give that hurt place in your heart to God, invite him in to bring healing and holiness.

And then there are the sexual issues, the holiness we need deep in our sexuality. I went back, one by one, and confessed to God my sins involving girls over the years—the ways I used them, the sexual intimacy that was not mine to have there. Sometimes we have to be very specific to find the cleansing and relief we long for, going back and renouncing specific events, inviting the blood of Christ to cleanse our every sin away, that our sexuality may be made holy. We bring the cross of Christ between us and every woman we've ever had an emotional or sexual relationship with (read Gal. 6:14). This would include affairs over the Internet, and with pornography, and every misuse of your sexuality. And, brothers, if you are in an emotional or physical relationship with a woman other than your wife even now, you must walk away. You must walk away. No stalling, no excuse-making. You will not find healing, holiness, and strength until you do.

I also found that for a season I needed to pray before Stasi and I made love, asking Christ to come and make our marriage bed holy, and heal both our sexual hearts. Sometimes I would do this alone, and sometimes with Stasi. It made a *huge* difference.

And then there is the "live moment," when a beautiful woman crosses our path in person or in an image of some sort, and our hearts are stirred. How we handle that moment is critical. We do not surrender, we do not kill the longing. We give that very place over to Christ. That place in your heart, right there, right then, give to Jesus. Awakened by a beauty, we give that part of our hearts to God. This will take some time, and many repetitions. We've given it over to the woman so many times before, there is much recovering to be done. Again? Yes, again and again and again. That is how we are healed, made whole and holy and strong.

Finally, we must open our hearts to all the other ways God is bringing beauty into our lives. The beauty of a flower garden or moonlight on water, the beauty of music or a written word. Our souls crave Beauty, and if we do not find it we will be famished. We must take in Beauty, often, or we will be taken out by beauty.

Learning to be loved, and learning to love, learning to be romanced, and learning to romance—that is what this stage is all about. Not duty. Not merely discipline. But an awakening of our hearts to the Beauty and Love of God, and at the same time (we cannot wait until some later time), we offer our hearts as well—to God, to the women in our lives, to our sons and daughters, to others. This is a love story, after all. As William Blake said, "And we are put on earth a little space / To learn to bear the beams of love." Or, in Paul's words, "Be imitators of God . . . and live a life of love" (Eph. 5:1–2 NIV). He is a great Romancer, and you shall be also.

Father, I have so much to learn here. Teach me to be a lover. Open the eyes of my heart to all the ways you have been romancing me. Remind me what awakened my heart when I was young. Show me how you are wooing me even now. I give my heart to you. Heal the wounded lover in me. Forgive me all my sins and failures here. Come, and lead me in deep repentance and restoration. Teach me to love with a whole heart.

7 KING

The highest heavens belong to the LORD,
but the earth he has given to man.

—PSALM 115:16 NIV

PICTURE IN YOUR MIND'S EYE AN IMAGE OF A GREAT
warrior, a renowned champion, returning home from far-off
lands. His fame has long preceded him, and now the reports of
his feats are confirmed by the scars he bears, the remembrance of
wounds more noble than any tokens of honor. With dignity he
moves up the main causeway of the city, lined with the faces of
his people, the very people for whom he has fought bravely,
whose freedom he has secured. The warrior has returned after
years on the field of battle, returning only when triumph was
achieved and not a moment before. This is his homecoming, and
it is as a conquering hero he returns. Before him, at the head of
the street, stands the king, who is his father. The scene is both a

homecoming and a coronation. For the father-king will now hand the kingdom over to his son.

> Who is this coming from Edom,
>> from Bozrah, with his garments stained crimson?
> Who is this, robed in splendor,
>> striding forward in the greatness of his strength?
> "It is I, speaking in righteousness,
>> mighty to save." (Isa. 63:1 NIV)

> After he had provided purification for sins, he sat down at the right hand of the Majesty in heaven. . . . About the Son he says, "Your throne, O God, will last for ever and ever." (Heb. 1:3, 8 NIV)

It could be a passage from David's life, for he came to the throne after proving himself as a warrior. But I am referring to Jesus, of course, and while this is all quite true—biblically, historically—I'm afraid the power of it eludes us. Few of us have ever lived in a kingdom, under a king. Even fewer have ever met one. The scene of Aragorn's coronation from *The Return of the King* might help us imagine what a great king is like:

> And when the sun rose in the clear morning above the mountains in the East, upon which shadows lay no more, then all the bells rang, and all the banners broke and flowed in the wind. . . . Now

the Captains of the West led their host towards the City, and folk saw them advance in line upon line, flashing and glinting in the sunrise and rippling like silver . . . and upon either side of the Gate was a great press of fair people in raiment of many colors and garlands of flowers.

So now there was a wide space before the walls of Minas Tirith, and it was hemmed in upon all sides by the knights and the soldiers of Gondor and of Rohan, and by the people of the City and of all parts of the land. A hush fell upon all as out from the host stepped the Dunedain in silver and grey; and before them came walking slow the Lord Aragorn. He was clad in black mail girt with silver, and he wore a long mantle of pure white clasped at the throat with a great jewel of green that shone from afar; but his head was bare save for a star upon his forehead bound by a slender fillet of silver.

. . . Then Frodo came forward and took the crown from Faramir and bore it to Gandalf; and Aragorn knelt, and Gandalf set the White Crown upon his head, and said: "Now come the days of the king, and may they be blessed while the thrones of the Valar endure!"

But when Aragorn arose all that beheld him gazed in silence, for it seemed to them that he was revealed to them now for the first time. Tall as the sea-kings of old, he stood above all who were near; ancient of days he seemed and yet in the flower of manhood; and wisdom sat upon his brow, and strength and healing were in his hands, and a light was about him.

Jesus lived the days of his youth as the Beloved Son, secure in his Father's love. He matured as a young man working in the carpenter's shop, and through his time in the wilderness. And then he went to war, and as the great Warrior he rescued his people from the kingdom of darkness, threw down the dark prince, set the captives free. As Lover, he wooed and won the hearts of his bride. And now, he reigns as King. Thus the progression of his life as a man, and thus ours.

BORN TO RULE

We come now to the goal, in some sense, of the masculine journey, the maturity for which God has been fathering the man since his first breath—to be a king. To wield power, influence, and property in his name. It is as great and noble an undertaking as it is difficult; history makes that very clear. The reason for many of our miseries upon the earth in these days is that we have lost our kings. Yes, we find men in power, but they are not true kings. It is not through initiation that they have come to the throne, nor do they have the heart of a king. And that is a dangerous situation indeed, when a man is made king who is unfit to be one, and it has brought the ruin of many kingdoms—homes, families, churches, ministries, businesses, nations.

Paul says the whole creation groans for the revealing of the sons of God (see Rom. 8:19–21). For we were meant to rule the earth, and this world is in anguish until we, the sons of God, are all that we were meant to be, and in being that can rule upon the earth in blessedness. We must recover the king in a man. This is the role for which man was created. The first man, Adam, was given the earth to rule (see Gen. 1:28), and he was intended to be the beginning of a race of kings. "The highest heavens belong to the LORD, but the earth he has given to man" (Ps. 115:16 NIV). But Adam failed, abdicated the throne through his sin, so another Man was sent to restore the line. Jesus was also born a King, and destined to rule, as the angel said to Mary, "The Lord God will give him the throne of his father David, and he will reign over the house of Jacob forever; his kingdom will never end" (Luke 1:32–33 NIV). And where Adam failed, Jesus triumphed. He is, of course, now the Ruler of heaven and earth. The Son of God, ruling on his Father's throne.

You, my brother, are from that noble line. You are a redeemed son of Adam, now the son of God (1 John 3:1–2). You were born to rule, *and you were redeemed to rule*. Destined to become a king. "Do not be afraid, little flock, for your Father has been pleased to give you the kingdom. . . . And I confer on you a kingdom, just as my Father conferred one on me" (Luke 12:32; 22:29 NIV). Jesus redeems his brothers to share his throne, to rule in his name.

Consider the parable of the Minas, as but one example. A king goes away to receive a kingdom. He appoints his servants to take care of his estate while he is gone. Upon his return, he rewards those who ruled well in his absence by giving them even greater authority: "Take charge of ten cities" (Luke 19:17 NIV). This is also the message of the parable about the sheep and goats. The sheep are the faithful ones, and their reward is a kingdom of their own. "Then the King will say to those on his right, 'Come, you who are blessed by my Father; take your inheritance, the kingdom prepared for you since the creation of the world'" (Matt. 25:34 NIV). A day is coming when the kingdom of God will appear in its fullness, when we will be given kingdoms of our own. We will rule, just as we were always meant to.

Meanwhile, God is training us to do what we're made to do. Every man is a king, for every man even now has a kingdom of sorts. There is some aspect of this world, however small, over which he has say. And as we grow in character and strength, in wisdom and humility, God tends to increase our kingdoms. He *wants* to entrust us with his kingdom.

THE HEART OF A KING

The great problem of the earth and the great aim of the masculine journey boil down to this: when can you trust a man with power? I remember Dallas Willard saying once that he believes the whole history of God and man recounted in the Bible is the story of God wanting to entrust men with his power, and men not being able to handle it. That was certainly true of Adam, and has proved true for most of his sons. The annals of the kings are, for the most part, a very sad record. Moses, David, Charlemagne, Lincoln—men like that seem hard to come by. My sincere hope is that as we embrace the masculine journey, submit to its lessons, learn again how to initiate men, we shall make good kings available once more.

But before a man is ready to handle power, his character must be forged. It might be said that all masculine initiation is designed to prepare a man to handle power. So let us return to MacDonald's thoughts on what God is after in raising his sons to full sonship. Consider this in light of a man, acting as a king:

> He will have them share in his being and nature—strong wherein he cares for strength; tender and gracious as he is tender and gracious; angry as and where he is angry. Even in the small matter of power, he will have them able to do whatever his Son Jesus could on the earth, whose was the life of the perfect man, whose works were those of perfected humanity . . . when we come to think with him, when the mind of the son is as the mind of the father, the action of the son the same as that of the father, then is the son *of* the father, then are we the sons of God.
>
> His children are not his real, true sons . . . until they think like him, feel with him, judge as he judges, are at home with him, and without fear before him because he and they mean the same thing, love the same things, seek the same ends. (*Unspoken Sermons*)

It is a beautiful work God is up to in a man, perhaps the most beautiful of all his works, and when this has taken deep root in a man's life, when he is well on his way to all MacDonald describes here as being true of him across the realms of his own life—certainly he will always have more to yield—but when this is true of a man more often than not, then is he ready to become a king.

It is a matter of the *heart*, my brothers. There are many *offices* a man might fulfill as a king—father of a household, manager of a department, pastor of a church, coach of a team, prime minister of a nation—but the *heart* required is the same. "The king's heart is in the hand of the LORD; he directs it like a watercourse wherever he pleases" (Prov. 21:1 NIV). The passage is often used to explain the sovereignty of God, in that he can do with a man whatever he well pleases. Certainly, God is that sovereign. But I don't think that's the spirit of this passage. God rarely forces a man to do something against his will, because God would far and above prefer that he didn't have to, that the man *wills* to do the will of God. "Choose for yourselves this day whom you will serve" (Josh. 24:15 NIV). What God is after is a man so *yielded* to him, so completely surrendered, that his heart is easily moved by the Spirit of God to the purposes of God.

That kind of heart makes for a good king.

Most of the men I know in some position of power and influence are not holy enough to handle even what they do have, and they are doing damage as we speak. They operate out of their business training and "principles of leadership," they operate out of a great deal of their own brokenness, but they do not, on any sort of regular basis, check in with God, submit to him, live as a man yielding his plans to him.

Watch how Moses leads Israel out of bondage, and guides them to the Promised Land. Notice how every chapter telling the story of the Exodus begins, from chapter 6 to chapter 14: "Then the LORD said to Moses . . ." (NIV), and the rest of the chapter is Moses doing what God told him to do. Is this how the men you know run their corporations, their churches, their families? I'm stunned by how little daily guidance Christian men seek from God. They have a good idea, and they just go do it. Not the great kings. Look at David. "In the course of time, David inquired of the LORD. 'Shall I go up to one of the towns of Judah?' he asked. The LORD said, 'Go up.' David asked, 'Where shall I go?' 'To Hebron,' the LORD answered. So David went up there . . ." (2 Sam. 2:1–2 NIV). In his heart, and in his daily practice, David is a man yielded to God. He is called, may I remind you, a man after God's own heart. (Learning to walk in this sort of intimacy is a good part of our initiation, but it begins with a yielded heart.)

Beyond question and without a doubt, this is the way Jesus lived. "For I did not speak of my own accord, but the Father who sent me commanded me what to say and how to say it. I know that his command leads to eternal life. So whatever I say is just what the Father has told me to say" (John 12:49–50 NIV). Jesus could have asserted his own will; he certainly had the power to do so, and the talent, and we might add he also could be trusted to do so. But no—he was yielded to the Father, in all things. Regardless of age, position, or natural abilities, a man is ready to become a king only when his heart is in the right place. Meaning, *yielded to God*.

ON BEHALF OF OTHERS

When the righteous thrive, the people rejoice;

when the wicked rule, the people groan. (Prov. 29:2 NIV)

Let us return again to *The Kingdom of Heaven*, to Balian's initiation. Following his father's instructions, Balian arrives in Jerusalem and reports to king Baldwin, who in turn sends Balian to protect the Pilgrim Road leading to the Holy City. "All are welcome in Jerusalem—not only because it's expedient, but because it is right." Balian rides out with his men to what was his father's estate there— a small farm settlement centered around a castle, like many medieval hamlets, only this one is out in the middle of the desert, more dust than anything else. Balian sets about making the place a refuge of life. What is needed is water, so he has the men dig wells, build aqueducts. Sybilla stops in on a visit, and when she sees him out there in the fields with his workers, sleeves rolled up, she asks, "Would you make this like Jerusalem?"

Beautiful. Exactly. That is what a good king does—he uses all he has to make his kingdom like the kingdom of heaven for the sake of the people who live under his rule.

I love the mission scenes in the movie *The Mission*, the story of young Spanish Jesuit priests bringing Christianity to the Indian tribes in South America, rescuing them from Portuguese slave traders. The missions they create in the jungle become outposts of freedom and life, little kingdoms of heaven where the native peoples thrive, creating cottage industries, schools, a music academy. They usher in a sort of golden age for the tribes, willing to put their lives on the line to serve the weak and vulnerable.

Or take the scene in the Civil War film *Glory*, about an all-black regiment of Union soldiers led by a young white officer. His troops need shoes, and the shoes are being "held up," intentionally, in the offices of the petty tyrant running supplies. That man is the classic picture of a king using his small authority to grab some comforts for himself, pillaging local farms to line his storehouse with treasures. The young captain takes a squad of his best soldiers, goes into the office of the little martinet, acts like a warrior, puts the poser in his place, and returns to camp with a wagonload of shoes. And his men begin to trust him.

There is Jean Val Jean, the criminal ransomed by the fierce love of a priest in *Les Misérables*. He goes on to become a great man, a king, in fact mayor of the town and owner of the tile factory. He uses his company to provide a sanctuary for young single women, bringing them off the streets to work in the tile lines. By employing them, he acts as that "oak of righteousness" described in Isaiah 61, and under his strength the vulnerable find refuge.

"And David knew that the LORD had established him as king over Israel and had exalted his kingdom for the sake of his people Israel" (2 Sam. 5:12 NIV). For the sake of his people. That is why a man is given a kingdom. We are given power and resources and influence *for the benefit of others*.

THE TEST OF A KING

Too many men, having reached this point in their journey—or rather, finding themselves kings even though they have *not* taken the masculine journey—seize the opportunity to make life good . . . *for themselves*. The average man in his forties or fifties comes into a little power and influence, a little discretionary cash, and he spends it making himself comfortable. He buys himself a lounger and a big-screen TV. He goes out to dinner, joins the country club, takes more expensive vacations. He works if he has to, but the purpose of his labors is only to build his savings so that he can lead a life of leisure. Is it not so?

There is a sense of entitlement that seems to come with the forties and fifties. The man has worked hard to get here, and something in him says, *Hey—I've paid my dues. Now it's my turn to have some fun.* "Take life easy; eat, drink and be merry" (Luke 12:19 NIV). I think of the senior pastor who kept urging his congregation to sacrifice even more for the church's building campaign, while he went out and bought himself a new Mercedes. Or a businessman I know who, having built a successful company, laid the burden of its increasing stresses on the shoulders of his people while he went off to buy cars, vacation homes. For him, it was eat, drink and be merry, but for them it was more bricks, less straw. This is not why a man is given power and property.

> Jesus called them together and said, "You know that the rulers
> of the Gentiles lord it over them, and their high officials exercise

authority over them. Not so with you. Instead, whoever wants to become great among you must be your servant, and whoever wants to be first must be your slave—just as the Son of Man did not come to be served, but to serve, and to give his life as a ransom for many." (Matt. 20:25–28 NIV)

I'll be the first to admit, this is proving one of the greatest tests of kingship in my own experience. I thought I discovered I was selfish when I married. You don't buy things simply because you want them? You don't think a tent is a wonderful place to sleep? To live in the constant company of another human being whose approach to life is different from the one you've been honing for years is an epiphany. Then children came along, and brought the revelation to a whole new level. I had no idea how precious sleep was to me. Or moments of silence each day. Treasures you can kiss good-bye when you shove off into parenthood. Even still, there seem to be inner resources available to help a man sacrifice when it comes to his family, though he might have to dig rather deep to find them on a daily basis. Then I became a king, or at least, I came into the stage of king, and discovered how very small the circle of my generosity naturally extends. Those inner resources seem to wear thin when it comes to people in general.

But that is the true test of a king. Simply put, the test is this: *What is life like for the people under his authority?*

Really. It's that simple. What is life like for the people in his kingdom?

Have a look at his wife—is she tired, stressed out, overlooked? What about his children—are they flourishing? How much energy does he spend simply getting his children to behave, versus understanding their hearts and looking for ways to bless them? Talk to the people who work for him—do they feel they are simply building *his* kingdom, or that he is serving them? Are they growing in their own talents and abilities, joyful because they are cared for, given a place in the kingdom? If he is a pastor, look at his congregation—are they enjoying the genuine freedom and life Christ promised? Or is the unspoken system of the church one of fear, guilt, and performance?

When you look at the lives of the bad kings—men like Saul, or Herod, characters like Denethor and Commodus in *Gladiator*—the contrast becomes clear. Life is all about them. The kingdom revolves around their happiness. You know they didn't wake each morning to ask themselves, "What good can I do for others today with the power and wealth I have?" But that is the question a good king asks. It requires a holiness most men simply don't desire.

Order, Protection, and Blessing

A good king brings order to the realm. God brings order out of chaos at the beginning of creation, and then he hands the project over to Adam to rule in the same way. Not as a tyrant or micromanager, but offering his strength to bring order to the realm. The reason we depict a king on his throne is to convey order, well-being. The king is on his throne and all is well in the world. Years ago, when I worked in Washington DC, the man in charge of the operation never came to a staff meeting. Not once. He let his team vie for themselves, and the result was pandemonium—everyone trying to stake out their own territory, defend their projects, reach for some glory. Every man for himself. That's what happens when a king won't rule. Likewise, a father who abandons his family throws them into emotional and financial chaos.

A good king also fights for the security of his kingdom, battling assault from without and sedition from within. That's why he must be a warrior first. Look at how tireless David is in bringing security to Israel's borders:

> In the course of time, David defeated the Philistines and subdued them. . . . David also defeated the Moabites. . . .
>
> Moreover, David fought Hadadezer son of Rehob, king of Zobah. . . . When the Arameans of Damascus came to help Hadadezer king of Zobah, David struck down twenty-two thousand of them. (2 Sam. 8:1–3, 5 NIV)

Think of Churchill, unyielding to the Nazis, and the pacifists in his own government who would not hold fast. Or Lincoln, and his unrelenting efforts to preserve the Union. A family with a good father feels protected. Spiritually, emotionally, financially, physically, he is the one to bring peace and covering to his family.

All this in order to bring blessing to his people. "From the fullness of his grace we have all received one blessing after another" (John 1:16 NIV). Nehemiah discovers that his people are being fleeced by their own officials, and demands their grain, oil, and lands be restored. He refuses even to take the booty allotted to his role. David insists that the plunder from the Amalekites be shared among every man, those who guarded the baggage and those who fought. A good king wants his people to share in the prosperity of the realm. Bad kings build their own offshore bank accounts.

THE COST OF BECOMING A KING

Augustine wept when he was made bishop of Hippo in North Africa. Those of you who have been kings will understand. There is a cost the king pays, unknown and unmatched by any other man.

A few months ago our team at Ransomed Heart was moved to fast and pray, over a three-day period, for the ministry. Whatever aims we might have had for the mission itself, God used the time profoundly on a personal level. To be more honest, the fast was, for me, a *rescue*. On the second morning I found some space to just listen and be with God. My journal and Bible spread out before me, I simply asked, "What do you want to say to me, Father?" *Josiah*, is what I heard. I'm thinking to myself, *Josiah . . . Josiah. Boy, that sounds familiar, but I can't place him. Is it one of the Minor Prophets?* I flip through the end of the Old Testament, looking for the book of Josiah. An embarrassing story to recount.

There is no book of Josiah, so I cannot find the book. I pull out a concordance and look up Josiah. There he is—in 2 Kings. I read the story of his life.

Josiah was a remarkable king and a remarkable exception in the sad annals of the kings. He led a period of tremendous spiritual and political reform in Judah. I was moved by his courage, his integrity, the purity of his life. Imagine this being said of your life: "Neither before nor after Josiah was there a king like him who turned to the LORD as he did—with all his heart and with all his soul and with all his strength, in accordance with all the Law of Moses" (2 Kings 23:25 NIV). No king like him, ever. I set the story down, and pondered why God had me turn here. "Yes, Lord. This is a good man, a man to admire and emulate. But I still don't know what you are after. What are you saying?" One word came in reply. *Rule.*

A long, deep sigh exhaled on its own, unbidden, unchecked, expressing some deep reaction within me. My left hand came up to rub my brow, slowly.

I knew what this meant. For the past several months—over the course of the summer—my heart had been drifting away from the ministry. I was so relieved to have had a respite from the pressures. All those relational minefields, tensions almost wholly brought on by spiritual warfare, yet those involved wanting to make them entirely real and the reflection of human issues, so I had to spend hours untying Gordian knots that could have been relieved in five minutes of prayer. The difficulty of leading in order to give others a platform and a say. Above all, the constant testing of the character of my own heart, with the adversary dogging, dogging, dogging my heels to accuse of pride or weakness or anything else that might dismay.

You kings will understand. My heart had drifted. I was quite willing to let the whole thing simply come to an end. Life would be so much easier. *Rule*, he says. Meaning, you don't get to leave the kingdom I have given you just yet. Meaning, I sense, there is a great deal more to be required of me. I thought I had sacrificed a good deal already for the advance of the kingdom. Now he is asking me to stay, and in staying, to sacrifice more. I think unless there is this profound reluctance to take the throne, a man does not understand the cost of what is being asked of him. You will be tested. On every conceivable front.

> Upon the king! Let us our lives, our souls,
> our debts, our careful wives,
> our children and our sins lay on the king!
> We must bear all . . .
> O hard condition,
> Twin-born with greatness, subject to the breath
> of every fool . . .
> What infinite heart's-ease
> must kings neglect, that private men enjoy! (*Henry V*)

You don't want to be a king. Trust me. It is not something to be coveted. Only the ignorant covet a throne. Augustine didn't want the job because he knew what it would cost him, and he felt a profound inadequacy to the task. He wanted a quiet, simple life. But he accepted the role on behalf of others. Becoming a king is something we accept only as an act of obedience. The posture of the heart in a mature man is *reluctance to take the throne, but willing to do it on behalf of others.*

THE WOUNDING OF THE KING

The king is wounded early in a boy when he is never given a territory of his own, when his territory is violated, or when his territory is too big for him.

A boy needs some territory to call his own. Does he get to choose what he wears—often? Does he have certain special toys that he does not have to let others play with? Is his room, especially, a little kingdom over which he has some say? Of course, a parent expects him to clean his room. I'm talking about choices of what color to paint it, what pictures he gets to hang on the walls. Do his parents and siblings have to knock before they enter? You might want to ask yourself, "The things that were precious to me when I was young—did I have any sort of control over them?" How else will he learn to rule?

If a boy has a domineering mother or father, it crushes the young king in him. He never gets to develop his own willpower and determination. For the king is also wounded early in a boy when his boundaries are violated. As Bly says:

When we are children our mood gets easily overrun and swept over in the messed-up family by the more powerful, more dominant, more terrifying mood of the parent.... If a grown-up moves to hit a child, or stuff food into the child's mouth, there is no defense— it happens. If the grown-up decides to shout, and penetrate the child's boundaries by sheer force—it happens. . . . When our parents do not respect our territory at all, their disrespect seems overwhelming proof of our inadequacy. (*Iron John*)

Sexual abuse would be among the worst violations, for the child is invaded and cannot make it stop. How then can he (develop a sense of sovereignty over his life, a confidence that he can assert his will, protect his boundaries? The child becomes accustomed to being run over, demanded of, used.

I said in chapter 1 that a boy is also wounded when he is made a king too soon, as often happens when the father abandons the family. Sometimes the father will even say, "You're the man of the house now," a terrible burden to lay on a boy. His shoulders are not nearly big enough for that, and won't be for a long time. Sometimes the mother does it, unintentionally, as she looks to the boy to become her companion, help her navigate life without a husband. Sometimes the boy will just take it on himself. It happens also when the boy has a weak father. It is an awful thing when you are five, or fifteen, or even twenty-five, to be the strongest man in your world.

Young men are wounded by kings who betray them, and the

wound often causes them to resent all kings and the role of king. Perhaps this is why so many young men today do not want to enter the stage of king, and think that they are more righteous for it. We often make young men kings too soon as well. The senior pastor leaves, and the church makes the youth pastor senior and he is twenty-five. Business schools give young men the impression that an MBA qualifies them to become a king, also in their twenties. The young man has barely learned to be a warrior, may never have been a cowboy.

Does this mean a young man cannot become a king? No. Josiah was twenty-six when he began his reforms, and he ruled well. But I would say that a young man should not be made king over too great a kingdom. He should be a manager before he becomes a vice president, and only after those stages should he become president. *If* he finds himself in the role of king as a younger man, he should *not* forsake the other stages of the journey, for he will need all they have to teach him and develop in him. It is not the *season* of the king for him, but of the warrior and lover, and it is at those stages he should live, looking to older men to help him fulfill the *office* of king.

Many of my readers will be older men, finding themselves kings and realizing they never received the initiation they needed as cowboys, warriors, or lovers. They feel a weakness inside, feel hard-pressed to rise up as king. That should alert them to go back and take the journey (more on this in the next chapter).

Kings are wounded when they are men as well, sometimes

wounded right out of being a king. There is betrayal—as David experienced with Absalom. It happens so many times, the enemy using people to try to bring down the kingdom, and mostly, to dishearten the king. Listen to Paul: "At my first defense, no one came to my support, but everyone deserted me. May it not be held against them" (2 Tim. 4:16 NIV).

Sometimes a king is forced out of his kingdom, as David was by Saul, and later by Absalom. He might be forced into early retirement. In other cases a good man more than ready to become a king is passed over for a promotion, and the job is handed to a younger man. You can be assured that the enemy will do whatever he can to keep a man from rising up as king. He will tempt, dishearten, assault—as he did Adam, Moses, David, and Jesus.

Whatever has diminished your heart as a king, or toward the king, you must not let it win. It is as a king you were born, and it is as a king you must rise. There is great good to be done, and many people to rescue—all that we are missing are the kings of the earth.

Father, it is with some hesitation that I ask this—but still, I ask that you come and take me into this stage, initiate me here, when the time is right for me. Show me how the king was wounded in me as a boy, as a young man, and in my adulthood as well. Show me where I've acted weakly, abdicating my authority. Show me where I've been a tyrant. Show me also where I have ruled well. Let me see what life is like for those under my rule, and, by your grace, let me become a great king on behalf of others. I give my life to you. Give me the heart and spirit of a man yielded to you. Father me.

RAISING THE KING

Adam was given the earth to rule, but when the test came—he folded. He didn't speak, didn't act on Eve's behalf. Satan was there, attacking his wife, threatening the whole kingdom, and Adam didn't do jack squat. He fell through his *acquiescence*, through his silence and passivity. That was how Satan became "the prince of this earth," as Jesus called him. And why John said, "The whole world lies in the power of the evil one" (1 John 5:19 NASB). Might I point out that many men fail as kings through abdication, through some sort of passivity? They refuse to take the role, or they refuse to make the tough decisions. Refuse to lead their people in battle. They look for a comfortable life.

The other extreme, after Adam's fall, is tyranny. Kings like Pharaoh and Saul and Herod. Men who use their power in order to control and manipulate. The pastor who won't share the pulpit with anyone. The CEO who won't take advice. The father who keeps his family cowed in fear. If a man would be a good king, he would do well to keep in mind these two extremes.

The earth was given to man, but Satan usurped the throne, as Scar does in *The Lion King*, as Commodus does in *Gladiator*, as does Absalom, who seized David's throne. Jesus came to win it back—to throw down the usurper, to break the claims of his rule, which were based entirely upon the sin of man. Through his absolute obedience to God and through his sacrificial death, he did indeed break every claim Satan might make to the kingdoms of this earth (see Col. 2:13–15). Now, "all authority in heaven and on earth has been given" to Jesus (Matt. 28:18 NIV).

And you, my brother, have been given that same authority. "And God raised us up with Christ and seated us with him in the heavenly realms" (Eph. 2:6 NIV). To be seated with Christ in the heavenlies means that we share in his authority. He makes it plain in Luke 10:19: "I have given you authority . . . to overcome all the power of the enemy" (NIV). Learning to live in this authority, to bring the kingdom of God to our little kingdoms on earth, that is what it means to become a true king.

In the scene I described earlier from *Kingdom of Heaven*, where Balian is given the oath and sword of a knight, his father also confers upon him his authority. Godfrey, baron of Ibelin, is about to die. His final act is to remove a ring from his finger and give it to Balian, a symbol of his authority passing now to his son. He is literally giving his kingdom to his son. "Rise a knight," his father's aide says to Balian, "and baron of Ibelin."

This, my brother, is what has happened to you through the work of Christ. Let me repeat, for this understanding about the kingdom of God is not broadly explained in the church just now. Adam (and all his sons, including you) was given the earth to rule. Born a King. He abdicated that authority to Satan through his sin and fall. But Jesus came and won it back, the Father giving all authority on earth to him. Jesus in turn shares that authority with us, gives us his authority, to rule in his name. For as he said, the Father is delighted to give us the kingdom (Luke 12:32). The course of a man's life is coming to the place where he can be made a king in his experience, where all that Christ has bestowed can be *realized* in the man's life.

Fathered into Kingship

I had been avoiding the issue for too long. We needed a new car. Stasi was driving a used Honda, which we'd bought back in the early nineties when we only had Samuel, and him in a car seat, and now we had three boys lined across the backseat and things were getting more than cramped. Even a trip to the grocery store was an Olympic event. It was like putting three prizefighters in a phone booth. Constant antagonism. Besides, the odometer read something above 150,000, the oil leaked, and okay—we needed a new car.

Still, I hesitated. Not just because Stasi wanted a minivan, and it took all the kindness and generosity in me to agree, but because something in me felt totally inadequate to be buying a car. I was thirty-five, and had never purchased a new car. Up to this point, all the cars I had bought were from friends. Going on my own to the dealer felt like a test of manhood, and I felt completely intimidated. But I sensed God asking me to do this, knew it was the loving thing to do for Stasi and for the family (a king rules for the sake of others). We test-drove vans, and then Stasi left me to do the negotiating. I felt about ten years old inside. *Hang in there*, the Father said. *You can do this.* For two hours—it seemed two days— I ran the gauntlet, and came out on the other side with the van she wanted in the color she wanted and for a pretty decent price.

The time came to write the check and close the deal, and once more my heart needed reassurance. *Is this really the right thing to do, Father?* I asked. *Yes.* So I wrote the check, sealed the deal. I handed Stasi the keys, and as she pulled away, big smile on her face and the three hoodlums—generously separated in back, waving—I heard God say to me, *Well done.*

It was like the voice of a father I never had. I felt . . . as if something in me had matured.

Back in the chapters on the warrior I explained that the way God most often teaches a man to fight is to put him in situation after situation where he must fight. The same idea holds true in the time of the king—our Father will put you in situations where you will need to act decisively, and strongly, on behalf of others. The king-heart in us is formed and strengthened in those moments—especially in those moments of sacrificial decision, when we do put others before us, and in those moments of unwavering decisiveness, when we take a difficult stand against great odds or opposition.

If you are like most men, you'll feel like you're in way over your head in moments like these. But this is how our initiation unfolds in our daily lives, how we come to discover that we do have the heart of a king, *can* act like a king. Not perfectly, not every time, but more and more as our initiation develops the king in us. I think we all know that such nobility and integrity can be formed in a man only by the Spirit of God. The question to us is, *Will we let him?*

If I were to choose one quality above all others to guide a man into, so that he might become a good king, it would be friendship with God. For if he has this, it will compensate for whatever other deficiencies the man may have, and if he does *not* have this, no matter how gifted he might be, he will not become the king he could have been. One of the big lies of the king stage is the idea that now you ought to know enough to operate out of your own resources. Not true. You will be faced with new challenges, bigger challenges, and the stakes are *much* higher. Many lives hang in the balance when you are a king.

Return with me, then, to the passage from John's epistle describing the different levels of relationship with God that come with the different stages of a man's life, giving special attention to his words to "fathers," which in this case means mature men:

> I write to you, dear children,
>> because your sins have been forgiven on account of his name.
> I write to you, fathers,
>> because you have known him who is from the beginning.
> I write to you, young men,
>> because you have overcome the evil one.

I write to you, dear children,

because you have known the Father.

I write to you, fathers,

because you have known him who is from the beginning.

I write to you, young men,

because you are strong,

and the word of God lives in you,

and you have overcome the evil one. (1 John 2:12–14 NIV)

Notice that for the mature man, the fathers, the chorus does not change. Of them, the older men, the same refrain is used twice. I assume something significant is revealed in the repetition. Something stable is implied here, something established and unchanging. They are the ones who "have known him who is from the beginning." "Have," meaning it's been going on for some time now. "Known," meaning actual, personal, intimate knowledge, as a man knows his best friend. "Him who is from the beginning," meaning God. The fathers are the friends of God.

How many kings do you know who act as if they *know* God, in the manner that friends know one another? Precious few, would be my experience. I've sat in hundreds of ministry meetings, board meetings, high-level gatherings of leaders; I have known a number of very successful businessmen, and very rarely have I met a king who acts like a friend of God. To give but one example—very rarely will a leader stop in the middle of a deliberation and say, "Let's ask God," then do it, right then and there, and listen, fully expecting to hear from him. (Have you?) But wouldn't that be one of the natural expressions of intimate friendship with God, that familiar turning to him in the hours of each day? If he *is* there, don't you want to know his thoughts on the matter at hand?

Perhaps the single greatest weakness common to good men now acting as kings is that they do not walk with God. They have learned some principles of leadership, they have their market analyses, they have their opinions, and they try to govern by these alone. They are not bad men, per se. But they live by a practical agnosticism, even men who are leaders in the church. I promise you, you cannot master enough principles to address every situation you will meet. Is this the time to attack, or retreat? Can you trust this alliance, or is it a trap? Is now the time to increase the kingdom, or work to improve the realm you already have?

I urge friendship with God as essential for a king for two reasons. First, because a man in power is positioned to do great good or great damage, and he will not have the wisdom to address every situation. Humility demands he turn to God, and often. Remember—the heart of the king is yielded to God. "For I did not speak of my own accord, but the Father who sent me commanded me what to say and how to say it. . . . So whatever I say is just what the Father has told me to say" (John 12:49–50 NIV).

But there is an even deeper reason than expedience. This is what a man was made for. To be a king and not know God intimately is like a son who runs part of the family business, but never talks to his father. Yes, we are here to serve as kings. But that service was never meant to take the place of our relationship with God.

But of course, all this you will have learned, or will learn, as you accept the orientation that is the premise of this book: your life as a man is a process of initiation into masculinity, offered to you by your true Father. Through the course of that journey, in all the many events of the beloved son, the cowboy, the warrior, the lover, whatever else you learn you will learn to walk with God, for he is walking with you.

> Father, raise the king in me. Develop in me the heart of a king. Help me to rule well, in your name. Teach me to be a good king, like Jesus. Help me to rule well right where I am. But above all else, teach me to live as your friend. Open my heart to the ways you are speaking to me, and leading me. Show me how to cultivate an even deeper relationship with you. To be one with you, even as Jesus is one with you. In all things.

8   SAGE

The glory of young men is their strength,
gray hair the splendor of the old.

—PROVERBS 20:29 NIV

I NEVER PLANNED ON BEING A WRITER. IT WAS SOME-
thing I just sort of fell into. When I was still a beloved son, like
most boys, I didn't think much about growing up at all, but when
I did, my dream was to become Batman, then a cowboy like my
grandfather, then a NASCAR driver. When first I became a Christian
(around the age of nineteen), I thought I should go to seminary
and become a pastor, because at the time I knew I wanted to give my
life to God, wanted to change the world (as a young warrior) and
pastoring was the only category for Christian service I had. (Many,
many young men have felt the same, and struggled with the fact
because their gifts and desires lie in other places.) And, for too many
years, I had no idea what I should do with my life.

The writing thing came up over coffee one day as I sat with Brent talking about a lecture series we were giving on *The Sacred Romance*. He said, "I think we should write a book about all this—I think there are some people out there who would like to hear what we're saying." "Oh, jeez, Brent," I sighed, "I don't have time for that." I was working forty-plus hours a week *and* going to grad school, giving what was left of me (which often wasn't much) to Stasi and the boys. There was a long pause, and then Brent said, "Well, okay. I think we should, but if you don't want to . . . why don't you think about it?" I rose and walked out of the coffeehouse. It's funny how our destinies turn on such simple moments. By the time I'd gotten my old '71 Wagoneer to start, I'd changed my mind.

In the nine years hence I have had no formal mentor in writing, no earthly father to father me in this beautiful, awful, lonely calling, fraught with dangers. But the Father has fathered me, in so many known and unknown ways, and he has sent a sage or two along at just the right moment. For this book, that sage has been Norman.

To understand how sages can come to us—how Norman came to me—let me first describe how I write. My morning begins with a time of concerted prayer—not out of any great piety but out of pure necessity. (I am useless if I don't, lost in a fog.) Breakfast follows, after which I will deal with whatever immediate necessities I absolutely must, resisting the temptation to answer every e-mail and phone call. Thirty minutes at most. Then I give myself to a day of writing. My favorite place to write has been the loft of the barn on our ranch, so fitting to the subject of this book, and so fitting to writing anything at all, for as Annie Dillard said, writing is like working with a wild horse. "You have to go down and catch it again every morning."

But—alas—I could not always be there, nor even mostly be there, so much of this book has been written in my office at home. Either place, before I write I will do two things. First, I review the words God has given me in advance of writing, or in the process of writing, words and phrases jotted down on 3 x 5 cards. I've spoken in other places of how important I feel it is, before one embarks on any mission of significance, to ask God for words of counsel. "Advance words" is what I've come to call them, and the reason for asking *in advance* is that quite often, once the enterprise has begun, you can't see the forest for the trees, and getting clarity in the midst of it all is typically much harder than before the dust begins to fly. Eisenhower said that before battle, planning is everything, but once the fighting begins, war is chaos. You know this to be true.

One of the things God said in advance was *Together*, as in, let us do this together. "It is the Father, living in me, who is doing his work" (John 14:10 NIV). Which is, of course, what this whole book is about. There was also a Scripture I'd written down on one of those cards, which God had given me maybe a year before the start of this project. "Set up road signs; put up guideposts. Take note of the highway, the road that you take" (Jer. 31:21 NIV). At the time I felt I was to take note of the verse itself, but it didn't make a lot of sense to me until I began this book, on the stages of the masculine journey. Then it had all the twang of the Spirit, like a shot from a bow. God also gave a very kind word: *the Gospels are not comprehensive*, for it spoke to my fear that I am not saying enough, overlooking crucial topics at every turn. I thought, *That's true—the Gospels don't read like a book of systematic theology*, and it gave my heart rest. There are other advance words I treasured as well, on my little white cards—but I won't tire you with them all. I'm trying to get to my point about the sage.

Next, I will sit down and take a long drink from the work of a better writer than I, to remember what good writing is like, to let it seep into my bones and strengthen me, just as years ago I would watch my master work the samurai sword before I took it up myself. For this book, God put into my hands (rather serendipitously) a wonderful work by Norman Maclean, author of *A River Runs Through It*. Late in life—in fact right up to the moment of his death—Maclean wrote another book, *Young Men and Fire*, a sort of detective story/Western on the Mann Gulch fire in Montana in 1949, which claimed the lives of thirteen young smoke jumpers. It is masterful in many ways (*The New York Times* called it "a magnificent drama of writing"), and I drew so much from its style, pace, prose. The effect of Norman Maclean's words, his posture, his life poured out on those pages cannot be fully described.

Thus Maclean was my sage in writing this book. I sat at his feet.

(An important reminder that mentors and fathers need not be physically present, nor even still living.)

Maclean was seventy-four when he began work on *Young Men and Fire*, and it was, for him, essential to what he called his "anti-shuffleboard philosophy," his defense against simply fading away with age. After hitting one of many obstacles in his research, Maclean recounted:

> I sat in my study making clear to myself, possibly even with gestures, my homespun anti-shuffleboard philosophy of what to do when I was old enough to be scripturally dead. I wanted this possible extension of life to be hard as always, but also new, something not done before, like writing stories. That would be sure to be hard, and to make stories fresh I would have to find a new way of looking at things I had known nearly all my life, such as scholarship and the woods.

Maclean was in his eighties when he wrote this—the research for the book requiring years of inquiry—and yet he wants to make his life *harder*? *Fresher*? I am amazed. This is the point at which most men retire to Sun City, spend their days at bingo or in front of the History Channel. Maclean undertakes a very difficult book, hoping in part that it "might save me from feeding geese." This is the heart of the sage—to make his greatest contribution with the last years of his life.

Because it claimed the lives of more smoke jumpers than any

previous fire, the Mann Gulch fire was immediately clouded in controversy, and by the time it was finally extinguished many important facts had already been "lost" by the U.S. government, which, Maclean notes wryly, "sometimes, of course, hides things to save its own neck and sometimes seemingly just for the hell of it." Digging up the truth proved exhausting. A Montana native, Maclean made several trips into the rugged mountains where Mann Gulch lies, his last when he was seventy-seven. The recorded heat in Helena that day was 94, and forest service experts put the temperature in Mann Gulch at 120 degrees. "On my way back I quit worrying about dying from a heart attack. Even before I reached the top of the ridge, death from dehydration seemed more immediate . . ."

Maclean's anti-shuffleboard philosophy has given us a great contribution—to literature, to those whose lives were shattered by the Mann Gulch fire, and to the study, and therefore prevention, of especially devastating forest fires. His determination also gives us, I hope, great inspiration for the sage. In notes he compiled for a preface to *Young Men and Fire* (the book was published posthumously, Maclean giving himself to the work to his last breath), the old sage writes this:

> The problem of self-identity is not just a problem for the young.
> It is a problem all the time. Perhaps the problem. It should haunt
> old age, and when it no longer does it should tell you that you
> are dead.

As I get considerably beyond the biblical allotment of three score years and ten, I feel with increasing intensity that I can express my gratitude for still being around on the oxygen-side of the earth's crust only by not standing pat on what I have hitherto known and loved. While the oxygen lasts, there are still new things to love, especially if compassion is a form of love.

THE STAGE

Humility demands I speak briefly here, for I have not lived this stage, and over the course of my life I've known only a few who have. Thus my remarks must be more observation than experience. Whenever this is the case, it should give us pause. I'm recalling something I read from Oxford Bishop Richard Harries:

> One of the most remarkable religious publications this century was the book of sermons by Harry Williams entitled *The True Wilderness*. This spoke to millions because, as he avowed, there came a point in his life when he was unwilling to preach anything that was not true to his own experience.

That is the secret of a truly powerful messenger, who carries weight, whom God will use mightily. Can you imagine the effect if every pastor made the same vow? Too many men are far too willing to offer their thoughts on subjects in which they have no real personal experience—*especially* experiences of God—and their "wisdom" is not grounded in reality. It is theory, at best, more likely speculation, untested and unproven. At its worst, it amounts to stolen ideas. Such clutter fills the shelves of most bookstores. The sage, on the other hand, knows of what he speaks, for he speaks from his experience, from a vast reservoir of self-discovery. Thus they said of Jesus, "The people were amazed at his teaching, because he taught them as one who had authority" (Mark 1:22 NIV).

Thus, regarding the sage, I will be brief.

I would place the stage of the Sage as beginning in the waning years of the king, sometime between the ages of sixty and seventy. There comes a time when the king must yield the throne. This does not mean failure. It means it's time to become a sage, and let another man be king. Too many kings hold on to their thrones too long, and they literally fade away once they have lost them (which tells us they were drawing too much of their identity from their position). It will appear that at this stage a man's "kingdom" may be shrinking—he retires from his career position, perhaps moves into a smaller home or apartment, lives on a fixed income. *But*, his *influence* should actually *increase*. This is not the time to move to Ft. Lauderdale, "wandering through malls," as Billy Crystal described it, "looking for the ultimate soft yogurt and muttering, 'How come the kids don't call, how come the kids don't call?'" For now the man is a mentor to the men who are shaping history.

The biblical archetype would of course be Solomon, but I

often think of Paul, writing his letters from jail. Rembrandt gave us a wonderful painting of the old sage, candle burning low, head resting in his hand propped up by an elbow on the table, writing— what? Ephesians? Philippians? Colossians? I love his letters to Timothy in particular, the tone of a loving father to son, a sage to a young warrior and king. Certainly the great mythic archetype would be Merlin, without whom Arthur could never have been king. (A king needs a sage, and a good test of his humility is whether or not he has one and whether or not he listens to him.) C. S. Lewis resurrects Merlin in one of his great novels, *That Hideous Strength*, and the old Celt becomes counselor to a remnant of Christians in a desperate holdout against an evil power seeking to control the world. Lewis also gives us Dr. Cornelius, the half-dwarf mentor to Prince Caspian, and the Professor, in whose house the children find the wardrobe and by whose wisdom they are saved from the barrenness of reason and launched into the world of Narnia.

Knowing how hard it is to find a sage, you might for the time being draw strength and inspiration from those we find in books and film. Yoda is a classic sage: "Fear leads to anger, anger leads to hatred, hatred leads to suffering." There is also the wonderful old priest in *The Count of Monte Cristo*. "Here now is your final lesson: do not commit the crime for which you now serve the sentence. God said, 'Vengeance is mine.'" "I don't believe in God," replies Dantes. "It doesn't matter. He believes in you." The sage who saves Seabiscuit is the wise horse trainer Tom Smith, counselor to the old king Charles Howard and the young warrior Red. "I just can't help feeling they got him so screwed up runnin' in circles he's forgotten what he was born to do. He just needs to learn to be a horse again."

Balian loses his father before he reaches Jerusalem, but he is not left alone. At this point enters a knight who is also a priest, by whose counsel Balian navigates the treacherous political and religious terrain of Jerusalem during the Crusades. Balian, unable to hear from God, says to him, "God does not speak to me. Not even on the hill where Christ died. I am outside of God's grace." To which the compassionate priest replies, "I have not heard that." "At any rate, it seems I have lost my religion." "I put no stock in religion. By the word *religion* I have heard the lunacy of fanatics of every denomination be called the will of God. Holiness consists in *right action*. And courage on the part of those who cannot defend themselves. And goodness. What God desires is here," he says, pointing to Balian's mind, "and here," pointing to his heart. "And what you decide to do every day, you will be a good man. Or not."

Finally, there is Gandalf, the hero behind all the other heroes in *The Lord of the Rings*. To him everyone looks—the young cowboys, the warriors, and the kings. I believe he is the secret to the trilogy's success, for he embodies that mythic longing deep in all our hearts for a true sage to walk the road with us. Certainly he completes the stages of the masculine journey as portrayed in this epic. He is the first chosen by Elrond for the Fellowship of the

Ring, "for this shall be his great task, and maybe the end of his labors." And when Middle Earth has been made secure, Aragorn chooses to be crowned by him: "Let Mithrandir [Gandalf] set it upon my head, if he will; for he has been the mover of all that has been accomplished, and this is his victory."

Proverbs says, "The glory of the young is their strength; the gray hair of experience is the splendor of the old" (20:29 NLT). How necessary is gray hair (or any hair at all, some might ask with hope)? All of the sages I just mentioned had gray hair. Perhaps with the exception of Yoda, whose three hairs look green to me, and come from his ears (which might also be a comfort to you aging men). Can a younger man be a sage? Certainly, to some extent. Solomon was king when he wrote Proverbs. But then again, he was given an extraordinary gift of wisdom from God. Certainly Jesus was a Sage, for there is no teaching that even comes close to his insight and compassion. And he was just into his thirties. So yes, a younger man can offer wisdom, advice, experience, counsel—certainly that is what I've tried to do in this book.

And yet . . . there are some things we just cannot know or understand until we have passed through the years that gray hair signifies. Say you are going to war in the Middle East. Would you rather spend an hour with a young officer from West Point, valedictorian of his class, who wrote his dissertation on Middle East conflicts, or, would you want to spend that time with Norman Schwarzkopf? I rest my case. Just as you don't want a young man to become a king too soon, you don't want him to present himself as a sage too soon, either—whatever his credentials might be.

AND WHAT IS IT THAT A SAGE OFFERS?

We live now in a culture of *expertise*, so completely second nature to us that we don't give it a second thought. Cutting-edge advances in science and technology—ever sharpening, ever thrusting forward—are now available to anyone with an Internet connection. If our doctor gives us grave news, we naturally get a second and third opinion from specialists. Businesses regularly hire consultants—experts—to help them get the edge over their competitors, and churches have jumped on the bandwagon as well. It's become one of our shared assumptions, this reach to "find the expert," and I wonder if it's part of the reason we do not understand or recognize a true sage. In business circles experts are sometimes even called sages.

They are worlds apart.

A sage differs from an expert the way a lover differs from an engineer. To begin with, expertise quite often has nothing to do with walking with God, may in fact lead us farther from him. For the expertise of the specialist gives us the settled assurance that he has matters under control, and that we will also, as soon as we put our trust in him. That is why we love him. "The reason your church is not growing is because you're not marketing yourselves properly to your intended customers." On a human level, that might be true, might produce some results. But wouldn't it be better to inquire of God why the church is not growing? The psychology of expertise comes indistinguishably close to the psychology of the Tower of Babel. "We have matters under our control now. Expertise has given us power over our destinies." And we know how God feels about that.

Now of course, there is nothing wrong with expertise—per se. I'd be the first one to find the best heart surgeon in the country should my son need heart surgery. And yet, why is it that we seem to have so few sages in our midst, that most of us have witnessed the sage only in stories like those I've recounted? Is it that they don't exist, or might it be that our near-worship of expertise has pushed the sage to the sidelines? And what are we to make of the passage that tells us, "Everything that does not come from faith is sin" (Rom. 14:23 NIV)? Whatever, whenever, wherever we place our hopes and confidence in something other than God, that is sin. Given mankind's inexplicable reluctance to rely on God, and nearly limitless ability to rely on anything else, can you see how the culture of expertise actually plays right into our godlessness, despite all our protestations to the contrary?

The sage, on the other hand, communes with God—an existence entirely different from and utterly superior to the life of the expert. Whatever counsel he offers, he draws you to God, not to self-reliance. Oh, yes, the sage has wisdom, gleaned from years of experience, and that wisdom is one of his great offerings. But he has learned not to lean upon his wisdom, knowing that often God is asking things of us that seem counterintuitive, and thus his wisdom (and expertise) are fully submitted to his God. Humility might be one of the great dividing lines between the expert and the sage, for the sage doesn't think he is one. "Do you see a man wise in his own eyes? There is more hope for a fool than for him" (Prov. 26:12 NIV). Thus we might not know we have a sage at the table, for he will remain silent while the "experts" prattle on and on.

The experts impress. The sage draws us to God. He offers a gift of presence, the richness of a soul that has lived long *with God*.

Years ago some colleagues of mine—young warriors, all of us—were plotting a sort of overthrow of the bad king under whom we served. We held a dinner in the basement of a German restaurant so that we might talk in private with a sage who consented to meet with us. Surrounded by stone walls, the wine cellar, talking of revolution—it felt like a gathering of the French Resistance, or perhaps Luther and his fellows on the eve of the Reformation. The sage, I'm now certain, saw clearly our naïveté, and all our shortcomings. But he was kind, and immensely patient with us, not too quick to point out our many faults. Instead, I remember he offered us *hope*. "Perhaps what God has meant in all of this is simply to bring you men together." A wise word, one that deflected the revolution, yet granted us dignity, and hope.

You may not have a sage in your immediate vicinity, but you can seek them out.

As the ministry we started in 2000 began to take off like a wild horse, I found myself in desperate need of counsel. I sought out a well-known pastor, whose humility I will respect by leaving him unnamed. We sat in a café while I riddled him with questions about the growth of his own ministry and how he handled it. He said, "Of course, it is my joy to do this. But God has asked me to do certain things I did not want to do, and yet I did them because the kingdom needed it." That was the threshold I was about to step over—to accept the burden of becoming a king, a burden I did not want but felt God was asking me to bear. And while this old saint's counsel was immensely helpful to me, there was something more given during our two hours that even still I find hard to describe. To sit with a man who has walked with God some seventy-plus years, to be in the presence of a father, to have the eyes of a wise and gracious man fixed upon you, to have his heart willingly offer you affirmation and counsel—that is a sort of food the soul of a man craves. All my years of loneliness and fatherlessness came into stark contrast. I could have wept.

And there are the sages I have looked to who are still speaking through their works. Two years ago I was asked to take part in a conference in the Northwest and though I rarely agree to these things, I felt God would have me go. My reluctance was due in part to my demanding schedule, but more so from the intuition that I would be a fish out of water, that there were some serious differences between my convictions and those held by the conference organizers. As I left the house to head to the airport, I sensed the Spirit move me to bring along George MacDonald's *Unspoken Sermons* (from which I've quoted several times in this book). The holiness that he portrays in those pages is . . . beautiful. The best I have yet to find.

As I feared, the conference proved a tremendous challenge to me, if only in my inner life, and the nearly constant decisions I had to make to walk in integrity and holiness. The atmosphere was swirling with religious success (the most dangerous kind), and though I knew something was wrong, it was hard to name. I'd go back to my room and pull out MacDonald, turn to any page, and find there an anchor, an unyielding integrity, a call to something higher. This passage in particular saved me: "As soon as [any] service is done for the honour and not for the service-sake, the doer is that moment outside the kingdom." It stung, but its sting was so good, for it caused me to check my own motives in the whole affair.

I hope you have had the opportunity to sit in the presence of a genuine sage, for then you will know that there is an indescribable something that a seasoned man brings with his presence. It's more than just wisdom, much more than expertise. It is the weight of many winters.

I come back to Maclean's resolution to live his life to the full, to the end. "There are still new things to love, especially if compassion is a form of love." *Compassion.* That is a beautiful word. As I think on the sages I have known and loved, I realize, *Yes, that's it—that's what seems to undergird the counsel of a sage. It is his compassion.* There is something a man who has lived a full life carries with him that cannot be learned from a younger source, however smart that source might be. The wealth of his experience is part of it, an essential part. But I think you'll notice that true sages offer the wisdom they've gained through experience with a sort of humility and tenderness, a graciousness I believe is best described as compassion.

It is a matter of presence. A sage does not have to be heard, as a warrior might, does not have to rule, as a king might. There is room in his presence for who you are and where you are. There is understanding. He has no agenda, and nothing now to lose. What he offers, he offers with kindness, and discretion, knowing by instinct those who have ears to hear, and those who don't. Thus his words are offered in the right measure, at the right time, to the right person. He will not trouble you with things you do not need to know, nor burden you with things that are not yet yours to bear, nor embarrass you with exposure for shortcomings you are not ready yet to overcome, even though he sees all of that. For he is wise, and compassionate.

Undeveloped, and Wounded

The heart of a sage goes *undeveloped* when a man has been a fool for most of his life, either in the form of a refusal to take the journey, or a refusal to take note of the journey he has taken. That man made something other than maturity his aim—success, usually meaning pleasure, or safety, meaning the path of least resistance. This is the man who spends his golden years walking his dog or golfing. The fool may have seen many winters, but they do not seem to have had any other effect on him beyond fatigue, or perhaps cynicism. Scripture describes a fool as a man who will not submit to wisdom, a man who refuses to be taught by all that life has to teach him. "A fool spurns his father's discipline" (Prov. 15:5 NIV). Sadly, there are many aged fools, as anyone who has spent time in Congress, or the university, or in the bowels of religious bureaucracies knows. Gray hair does not a sage make. No doubt you have experienced that by now.

The heart of the sage is *wounded* when he is dismissed as a has-been, too old to have anything to offer. I recall a term I heard years ago, speaking of the men who led the church early in the twentieth century: "Yesterday's Men." At the time I liked the term. A young warrior itching for his moment, something in me said, *That's right—these guys need to move over. It's our turn.* In retrospect, I repent of my arrogance. For now, twenty years downriver, I hate that phrase. We need more men around who have lived through yesterday, seen it, and even if they haven't conquered it, they have learned from it. Young warriors will sometimes dismiss the older men in their lives because those men no longer yearn for battle, or simply because they don't come from "my generation." Thus the sixties adage, "Never trust anyone over thirty."

Insecure kings often dismiss the older men around them, send them into early retirement, threatened because the older men know more than they do. And our culture in the progressive West has dismissed the elderly for years now, because we have worshipped adolescence. Our heroes are the young and handsome.

The "winners." We've worshipped adolescence because we don't want to grow up, don't want to pay the price of maturity. That is why we have a world now of uninitiated men. Thus the heart of the sage is wounded when he is dismissed, or sent into exile, or Scottsdale, which is pretty much the same. No one seems to want what he has to offer, and he comes to believe after a time that it is because he has nothing to offer.

These, at least, are my observations. No doubt there are other ways the sage is wounded, and I will let them tell us as we seek them out. For we must seek them out, brothers.

Raising the Sage

The greatest gift you can give to a sage is to sit at his feet and ask questions. I remember how my grandfather on my mother's side would light up when I asked his opinion about *anything*, or simply to tell me stories of his life. He and my grandmother— both Irish Catholics, both passionate and opinionated, both with a taste for Irish whiskey—lived in a small apartment, a great deal of the time alone but for each other, and, after fifty-five years of marriage, they had reached a sort of cordial détente; for the most part my grandmother didn't want to hear his opinion on anything anymore. A prophet without honor in his own home. When I'd come in the summer he'd light up, shedding it seemed twenty years, and he'd walk faster and talk with enthusiasm, gesturing wildly, because he had a disciple eager to learn.

It's important that we ask because often in humility the sage will not offer until he is invited to do so. It's also important that we ask because quite often the sage himself is not aware of all that he knows. It is the *questions* that stir his soul, and memory, as a smoldering fire leaps to life again when stirred. In this way we can help to raise the sage.

Now, for you younger men, don't worry much about this stage, for it will come in due time. When you are young, commit yourself to take as few shortcuts as possible. Learn your lessons. Take note of all that God is teaching you. Submit to the journey. Be a student of the Scriptures. Hang out with the wise, living or dead, for that is how we, too, become wise.

As for you older men, if the sage has gone undeveloped in you because you didn't take the journey or take note of the journey you have taken, well, you'd better get busy, 'cause times a-wastin'. At this point you haven't years to go back and gather through many experiences all that you need; you had best walk closely with God, let him focus you on what he'd have you learn now. Some of you just need to be a beloved son. Or perhaps a lover. The wisest thing to do is to seek the communion with God that age and large amounts of time on your hands now allow for. The boy knows God as Father, the cowboy knows God as the One who initiates, the warrior knows God as the King he serves, the lover knows God as his intimate One, and the king knows God as his trusted Friend. The sage has a deep *communion* with God. This is a man, as Crabb described it, living on heaven's shore.

Those of you older men who have been wounded, or dismissed—have you made a vow never to offer again? I have seen something of how painful that can be. Seek the comfort and healing Christ offers. Let your heart be restored, for you *are* needed. Despite your wounds, I urge you to offer. We need you to offer. Resolve, as Maclean did, to live and to offer. This is also the story of George MacDonald, a prophet for the most part unwelcomed and unhonored in his time. His church ran him out because he unsettled them with his heart-centered theology and true holiness. His books did not sell all that well. His health suffered also. One of his best books (in my opinion) is *Diary of an Old Soul*, which begins,

> Lord, what I once had done with youthful might,
> Had I been from the first true to the truth,
> Grant me, now old, to do—with better sight,
> And humbler heart, if not the brain of youth;
> So wilt thou, in thy gentleness and truth,
> Lead back thy old soul, by the path of pain,
> Round to his best—young eyes and heart and brain.

I am not alone in being profoundly grateful that he did. Much of what we have received from C. S. Lewis is a result of MacDonald's choice, for he became Lewis's mentor of sorts, through his writings. In the spirit of MacDonald's prayer, what would you ask God for the strength now to do? What is on your heart? Remember, "The problem of self-identity is not just a problem for the young."

Consider yourself a sage, and ask yourself, "What would I love to now be my greatest contribution?" Position and power are highly overrated anyway. Let the kings shoulder those burdens. They are not your identity. What we need is your heart, and the life you've lived. Please—do not fade away.

Read *Tuesdays with Morrie*—the story of a young man and a sage, and then ask yourself, "How can I offer this?" There are many fatherless young men out there—find a way to draw them in. Teach a class. Take them through this book (provided that they've first read *Wild at Heart*—in fact, start there). Start a poker night, and invite four men to join you. Take some guys fishing, or to a cabin in the mountains. Call the younger men in your family who live out of state, and pursue relationships with them. Make yourself *available*—the questions will arise in time. Offer yourself to a king you know—your pastor, or youth pastor, a missionary serving overseas with whom you can correspond, or a young businessman. Serve on the board of your church, or the local board of education. Take up pen and paper. Tell your story. This is not the time to be feeding geese.

Think of what they said of Gandalf: "This shall be his great task, and maybe the end of his labors."

Father, I need you now, need you to the end of my days. I ask you to raise the sage in me. Help me to become a man of genuine wisdom and compassion. [For you younger men:] Show me the sages you have for me, both living and dead.

Help me find them, and sit at their feet. [For you older men:] Show me the men and women who need my counsel, and show me how to pursue them. Speak to me, Father, stir the fire in my heart. Show me what my contribution is now to be, and father me in making it with all my heart.

9   LET US BE INTENTIONAL

You have made known
to me the path of life.

—PSALM 16:11 NIV

ALL MASCULINE INITIATION IS ULTIMATELY SPIRITUAL.
The tests and challenges, the joys and adventures are all designed
to awaken a man's soul, draw him into contact with the masculine
in himself, in other men, in the world, and in God, as Father. I
make no distinction between taking a boy or a man on an adventure and, say, teaching that man to pray. The adventure—rightly
framed—can be a powerful experience of God. And prayer or
Bible study—rightly framed—is meant to be the same. Most boys
and men share the perception that God is found in church, and
that the rest of life is . . . just the rest of life. It's the old Gnostic
heresy, the division of the sacred and the profane. The tragedy of
this is that the rest of life seems far more attractive to them than

church, and thus God seems removed and even opposed to the things that make them come alive.

But as Christians, we believe God embraces the physical world, that he loves Creation as we do, pronounced it *very* good (Gen. 1:31), that he speaks through it and uses it to teach us many things. We've lost many boys and men from the church because we've given them an unspeakably boring spirituality, implying that God is most interested in things like hymnals and baptismal founts. We've made the spiritual very small, and sanctimonious, robbed and often effeminate. And yet, most of the stories of men encountering God in the Bible do not take place in church(!). Moses is met in the desert, in a burning bush. Jacob wrestles with God in the wilderness also, in the dead of night. David wrote most of his psalms out under the stars. Paul is met on the desolate dirt road *between* Jerusalem and Damascus. And most of the stories of Jesus with his disciples don't take place in church. Not even indoors.

We have got to recover the wildness of spirituality—especially masculine spirituality.

I say this because I know that many of my readers have done a good bit of time in the church, and they're wanting to know "Where's the Bible in all this? What about discipleship for boys and men?" The question proves my point—that we have lost both a noble view of the earth and how God uses it to disciple us— meaning, to train, develop, and make holy—and we have lost the wildness of masculine spirituality.

We must put ourselves into situations that will thrust us forward in our journeys. So much of our daily lives is simply routine, and routine by its very nature is *numbing*. Get out of it. Break away. I didn't get my time in the mountains with God this year, and not only did I miss it, but I can tell. My heart is not in the same place it would be in if I had; something is missing. The tank is half full. The connection is somewhat frayed.

God honors our intentionality as men, and while he will arrange for much of the journey, he asks us to take part as well, to *engage*. Ask, seek, knock, as the Scriptures urge. Though you may still feel very young inside, and at times our Father will be tender with those places, you are still a man and he will treat you like one. Be *intentional* about your own initiation into masculine maturity, as intentional as you would want to be toward your own sons, as intentional as you hope God is toward you. This is not a spectator sport.

No Fear

We parked our car at the Spanish Creek trailhead and began to gear up, double-checking backpacks, climbing gear, strapping helmets on the outside, filling Nalgenes with water, laughing nervously about what we were about to undertake. "It's ten miles in to base camp tonight. And over six thousand feet of elevation gain," I said. "So we're going to have to pace ourselves. I've heard this gets brutal." Our team was made up of Gary and his fourteen-year-old son, Nick, me and Blaine, and John Patten—an older and much more experienced climber we'd met through one of our retreats. When I began to think of a big climb that Blaine and I could do together, I asked John to come and be our guide. He's led more than thirty trips on the Grand. But that turned out to be just one of many divine twists in this story. We weren't headed into the Grand. We were headed into Kit Carson Peak, in the Sangre de Cristo Mountains in Colorado.

The choice was partly due to Blaine, and partly to God. The Grand is such a beautiful mountain and the Exum Ridge was such an exhilarating route, I thought we'd do it for Blaine's year as well. But when I broached the subject, he said, "That's Sam's mountain. I want to climb my own." Of course. You bet. You need your own mountain. So we began some research. There's a Web site that's been created on "The Classic Climbs of North America," including Denali, the Moose's Tooth in British Columbia, Devil's Tower, the Grand, and dozens more chosen for their beauty, challenge, and elegance of climbing. The Prow on Kit Carson caught our attention—a fin of rock ascending nearly a thousand feet with spectacular exposure, offering a climb similar in drama to the Exum Ridge but far less crowded.

I began to realize what I'd gotten myself into the night before we began our trek. John and I had all our climbing gear laid out on my living room floor, talking it all through to make sure we had what we needed. That is when a sinking feeling began to happen in my stomach. "We're going to have to climb in two teams," I said. John nodded. What we were realizing was that on a multipitch climb like the Prow, as the lead climber works his way up the face, he needs his partner behind him to climb up to him after a stretch and return the gear he's used to protect the route, so that he can use it again on the next pitch. If you tried to carry enough equipment to protect an entire thousand-foot climb, it would weigh close to seventy pounds. And then there was the issue of speed.

Lightning storms are common to Colorado most summer afternoons. We'd need to move fast to get up and off the peak by midday. Climbing as a group would be cumbersome. We would have to split up. Suddenly it began to add up, like when you do your taxes and realize you *thought* you'd given the government enough of each paycheck but now you see you didn't. You owe big-time. As the next most experienced climber, I was going to have to lead one of the teams. And, because John would lead a team of three, it made sense for Blaine and me to go first, because we would be moving faster. The realization kept repeating itself in my head: *I'm going to have to lead. Our team has to go first.*

At nearly every stage of our masculine journey, something in us needs to be dismantled and something needs to be healed. Often what needs to be dismantled is the false self, the poser, and the approach to life we've created to secure ourselves in the world. What typically needs to be healed are the fear and wounds beneath it, that fueled its construct. My invitation to John was purely an attempt to avoid being trip leader. Yes—I wanted my attention fully available to Blaine. But even more, I didn't know if I could lead this climb. Now I have to. What was being dismantled was my commitment to arrange life the way I wanted it, and I knew God was in it. It had that feeling of inevitability you get when you know God is closing in on you. What was going to need healing was an old issue with fear.

The hike into Kit Carson begins in high desert—pinion pines and juniper and cactus and heat. It must have been almost ninety degrees when we set out. Thank God—the trail crosses Spanish Creek seven times as it makes its way up the canyon toward the mountains, and the water was a welcome relief, even though the stream crossings were a little dicey with a full backpack. As you ascend you pass through Cottonwoods, and then into evergreen forest. After about seven miles we emerged from the timber to a magnificent view of the valley rising before us, and there, jutting out from the south side of Kit Carson, was the Prow. The name explains itself the moment you see it—a great mass of rock thrusting out into the valley, its sheer sides sweeping back toward the mountain from its outermost edge like the prow of a great ship. Even miles away, it looked daunting.

You can do this, I repeated to myself, repeating what God had said to me on the drive out that morning. While everyone slept in the car, I prayed. *Are you sure this is the right plan? I mean, we're talking death here.* The Father said, *You can do this.* That's all he said. I let several minutes pass, waiting for more. That was it. *Okay. I can do this.* We drove along in silence for a while and then I thought to myself, *Who is being initiated here?*

Between us and the high peaks lay hundreds of fallen trees,

killed by forest fire years ago and blown down in some storm, scattered all across our path. We picked our way through and over and sometimes under for another two hours. A grueling hike. Perfect. This is a quest, after all. Think The Lord of the Rings, think *Kingdom of Heaven*—what great story goes easily? It began to rain and I set a faster pace for camp. As we cooked dinner on our little Primus gas stoves, we talked one more time through the plan for the next day, then hit the sack. I stayed up late that night, reading trip reports in my tent by headlamp, poring over route descriptions for the fifth time. As if it would take my fear away.

Mist was swirling around the peaks the next morning as we made our way to the base of the Prow. Mist is beautiful, but not good for an ascent like this. Two other climbers asked if they might go before us, and because we acquiesced, our climb didn't begin until nearly 10:00 a.m. There was no way we would get off the peak by noon, and weather was swirling all around us. "We had better pray," someone said. And we did pray, asking God for a go or no-go. This is the best kind of discipleship, this real-time stuff, as we invited the boys to listen with us. "I hear a go," said Gary. "Me, too, said Nick." John nodded. "I heard 'Go,'" said Blaine." So had I, which could have come only from the Wild Goose, a name early Celtic Christians had for the Holy Spirit. We were starting late on an unknown climb in sketchy weather. Perfect.

You'll remember that crucial to the warrior is the ability to set your face like flint, to guard your heart and let nothing in. Not even fear. If you can keep your head about you . . .

The Prow is made of a kind of rock called conglomerate, a sort of hodgepodge of large and small stones held together by ancient clay. Wonderful for handholds, terrible for placing protection because there are no cracks. I'd read about the hairy run-outs on the Prow, the lead climber having to ascend forty to sixty feet past his last protection to find a crack in which to place a small nut. (The math for the lead climber is x 2, meaning, you fall twice the length of the rope to your last protection, because you have to fall to it and then past it that much again until—hopefully—it arrests your fall.) As one guidebook says, "The nature of this climb is abundantly clear at this point. Escape and protection are difficult," meaning, there is no way off but up, and as you go up, finding places to use the gear you brought proves elusive. "There is tremendous exposure in every direction, and the commitment increases with every pitch."

Blaine was marvelous, through all of it. Both he and Nick kept their spirits up, faced each pitch with courage, never let themselves give way to fear or uncertainty. As the day wore on, I could see thunderstorms building out in the San Luis Valley, and all I could do was pray they didn't come our way. On about the third pitch, my hands began to cramp badly, the muscles pulling them into the shape of a fist. *Do not give way to fear. You can do this.* I kept having to stop and pry my fingers open so that I could continue climbing, up into the mist, which continued to obscure the route and obscure me from Blaine. Thankfully, we had radios to communicate with each other. That is, till I kicked mine off a ledge.

We made the summit at 6:00 p.m., the time at which we'd planned on having been back in camp for hours and now making dinner. Blaine and I snapped a photo of ourselves, then checked in by radio with John. "It's marvelous climbing," I said. "You're going to love the last few pitches." "Congratulations on the summit," he radioed back. "We'll be there as quick as we can."

Climbing is wonderful practice for living. If you will choose to take the risk, it will be beautiful, exhilarating, and dangerous. Yes, at times it seems insurmountable. That is true for all of us. Blaine later told me that when he started up after me on the first pitch, he had to keep telling himself, *I've done this before. I've done this before. The only difference is the exposure.* Thankfully, climbing, like life, comes to us one piece at a time. You cannot take on the whole mountain at once, just as you cannot create a marriage at once. You make the next move, committed that your only plan is to do it. Much of it is unpredictable, like the weather, the lost radio, the unknown route itself. Many times on the Prow, Blaine and I had to do what is called a "running belay," where both climbers are climbing at the same time because the lead climber has extended the rope to its fullest and has not yet reached a good belay station himself. It's sketchy—like life, when you live it, versus trying to manage it.

Climbing takes you beyond your physical and emotional limits, as life will do. How else will we discover that there *is* more to us, that indeed God is our strength and our life? And, it doesn't always go well. I have been turned back from many summits because of weather or safety. My best friend was killed in a climbing accident.

Do we let these things stop us? When his son was killed in a mountaineering accident, Nicholas Wolterstorff wrote:

> But why did he climb at all? What was it about the mountains
> that drew him? I suspect that only those who themselves climb
> can really know. . . . How insipid it would be if every misstep,
> every slip of the hand, meant no more than a five-foot drop into
> an Alpine meadow. The menace is essential to the exhilaration of
> achievement. (*Lament for a Son*)

It's true. And something in a man responds.

Finally, at some point in your journey, you will be required to take the lead, even though you don't feel up to it. You can choose to do this yourself, or, God can force it upon you. It seems that just when we feel we've begun to get the hang of a certain stage, he calls us on to the next.

My favorite moments with Blaine on the Prow were when we sat side by side on a ledge about the size of a park bench, our legs dangling off the edge hundreds of feet above the start of the climb and more than a thousand feet from the valley floor. We'd clip into some protection and have a bite to eat, bonded by what we've done, and what we've yet to do.

> Before we part, a word upon the graver teaching of the mountains.
> See yonder height! 'Tis far away—unbidden comes the word,
> "Impossible!" "Not so," says the mountaineer. "The way is long, I

know; it's difficult—it may be dangerous. It's possible, I'm sure. I'll seek the way, take counsel of my brother mountaineers, and find out how they have gained similar heights . . . we know that each height, each step, must be gained by patient, laborious toil, and that wishing cannot take the place of working . . . and we come back to our daily occupations better fitted to fight the battle of life and to overcome the impediments which obstruct our paths, strengthened and cheered by the recollection of past labors and by the memories of victories gained in other fields. (Edward Whymper, *Scrambles Amongst the Alps*)

Our life *is* a quest, my brothers, arranged by our Father, for our initiation. There are gifts along the way to remind us that we are his beloved sons. Adventures to call forth the cowboy, and battles to train the warrior. There is Beauty to awaken the lover, and power on behalf of others to prepare the king. A lifetime of experience from which the sage will speak. The masculine journey, traveled for millennia by men before us. And now, my brothers, the trail calls us on. Remember this:

I will not leave you as orphans; I will come to you. . . . My Father will love him, and we will come to him and make our home with him. (John 14:18, 23 NIV)

Because we are the sons of God, we must become the sons of God. (George MacDonald)

EPILOGUE   WHERE DO I GO FROM HERE?

As the people of God stood on the brink of the Promised Land, poised to carry their journey forward, Moses issued a warning: "Only be careful, and watch yourselves closely so that you do not forget the things your eyes have seen or let them slip from your heart as long as you live" (Deut. 4:9 NIV). The seasoned old sage knew human nature well, how forgetful we are, what a disaster it would be for them to lose hold of all that God had been teaching them. It is a warning that echoes down through the ages. Don't forget. Don't let this slip away.

There is *so* much set against a man getting the breakthrough he needs in his life, and hanging on to the breakthrough once it comes. We live in a world at war, but much of the battle is so subtle we often don't see its dangers until long after we've fallen prey to them. The busyness of our culture, the distractions, the way the Church rushes from one fad to the next—all of it comes together to steal from a man the very things he needs to hold on to. And so I urge you, *stay with this*. The masculine journey is the central mission of your life.

Let me offer some counsel for your journey now. As my editor Brian was working through the book, he told me he found that it took a second reading to really begin to take in all that is written here. So the best thing you could do at this point is *read it again*. There is no way you have gotten all that God has for you in one pass—the scope of the journey is too great, and our needs for healing and initiation too great to perceive all at once. As I recommended in the introduction, use the *Fathered by God Manual* as you make your second pass through. It's available as a free download at www.ransomedheart.com/fatheredbygod. Better still, get a few guys together and do it as a band of brothers.

Then what? Come to Ransomedheart.com and you will find there many tools and maps for your initiation. Like our audio series, *The Hope of Prayer,* and *The Utter Relief of Holiness.* We offer camps and retreats for men, and podcasts. Come, and continue the journey!

Finally, beware the culture of busyness, and its unending craving for "the next thing." There are a lot of movements out there in Christendom right now, and they are not all of the same heart. Stay with the journey you've begun here. Don't let this slip away. Of course, you know now that my counsel will always first and foremost be, "Ask God." He knows what you need next. Ask him what he has for you—what friends, what adventures, what battles, what help he has in store. Be intentional. "Those who are led by the Spirit of God are sons of God" (Rom. 8:14).

ACKNOWLEDGMENTS

MY DEEPEST THANKS TO SAMUEL, WHO HELPED IN THE research for this book; to Brian Hampton, whose editorial strength was gracious and brilliant; to the whole team at Nelson working to bring this together; to Curtis and my allies at Yates & Yates who vigilantly guard my flank; and to the many men whose lives have brought to me the understanding and hope offered in this book.

WHERE DO I GO FROM HERE?

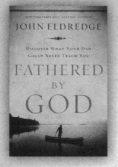

Available exclusively as a free download at www.ransomed heart.com/fatheredbygod

FATHERED BY GOD MANUAL

The path to manhood is a journey of discovery and experience, trial and adventure. In the *Fathered by God Manual* available exclusively as a free download at www.ransomedheart.com/fatheredbygod, John Eldredge comes alongside those men who long to have a guide to lead them through this rite of passage, this masculine initiation. Filled with personal stories, illustrations from popular movies and books, and probing questions, this manual will set you on a heart-searching expedition to become the man God sees in you.

WILD AT HEART

Every man was once a boy. And every little boy has dreams, big dreams. But what happens to those dreams when they grow up? In *Wild at Heart*, John Eldredge invites men to recover their masculine heart, defined in the image of a passionate God. And he invites women to discover the secret of a man's soul and to delight in the strength and wildness men were created to offer.

Hardcover—ISBN 0-7852-6883-9
Trade Paper Edition—ISBN 0-7852-8796-5
Abridged Audio in 3 CDs—ISBN 0-7852-6298-9
Abridged Audio in 2 Cassettes—ISBN 0-7852-6498-1

CAPTIVATING

John Eldredge and his wife, Stasi, show women how to reveal their three core desires—to be romanced, to play an irreplaceable role in a grand adventure, and to unveil beauty—and are encouraged to restore their feminine heart. In the style of *Wild at Heart*, women are shown the possibilities their dreams can afford and men are given a glimpse into a woman's soul, where they can see the strength and beauty God placed there for a reason.

Hardcover Edition—ISBN 0-7852-6469-8
Abridged Audio on 3 CDs—ISBN 0-7852-0909-3
Spanish Edition *(Cautivante)*—ISBN 0-8811-3278-0

THE MASCULINE JOURNEY

What does it mean to become a man? More importantly, *how* does a boy and a man become a man—and know that he is one? There was a journey of masculine initiation that men followed for centuries. But we lost that—at the same time we lost a father-centered view of the world and lost our own fathers. But there is hope. In this series that inspired *Fathered by God*, John Eldredge reveals how God comes to a man as Father, and invites him on a journey of masculine initiation. John walks through the stages of the journey—from Boyhood to Cowboy, the Warrior, the Lover, the King, the Sage—and shows us how we can offer this to our sons as well.

DEVELOPING A CONVERSATIONAL INTIMACY WITH GOD

Developing a Conversational Intimacy with God is the first volume in the CONVERSATIONS WITH RANSOMED HEART series. This new audio series takes you deeper into the issues that affect your heart and relationship with God. This first volume explores why an intimate walk with Christ is part of the normal Christian life. Christ longs to speak, and it is our right and privilege to hear His voice. If you long for more in your relationship with God, this CD will help you understand *how* and *why* we are invited into this closest of fellowships with Him and how you can respond to Him.

THE FOUR STREAMS

Christ wants to do more for us than simply forgive. Look at the miracles He did: the blind saw, the lame walked, the dead were raised to life. Christ was trying to show us something. He wants to restore us. If you will look again at the ways in which Christ ransoms people, the means by which he makes a man or woman come fully alive, you'll find he offers his life to us through four streams. Those streams are Discipleship, Counseling, Healing, and Warfare. Think of them as Walking with God, Receiving God's Intimate Counsel, Deep Restoration, and Spiritual Warfare. To discover for yourself that the glory of God is man fully alive, you must drink deeply from the four streams that Christ sends to you.

Lots more great resources from John Eldredge at www.ransomedheart.com

Now on DVD
New York Times best-selling author
John Eldredge unveils six stages men must
Complete to become who God
Designed them to be.

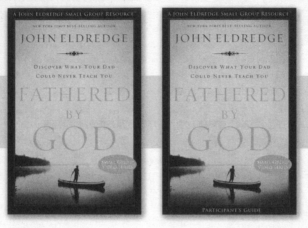

DVD   Participant's Guide

Using a men's small group setting, John takes users through six stages a man goes through as he matures in life and faith. Each session includes a 8–10 minute opening from John followed by 12–15 minutes of a men's small group, led by John, in a "Band of Brothers" way. Inspiring and challenging for men and the women in their lives, the Fathered by God DVD Small Group Video Series delivers a way for men to forge companionship with God the Father while undergoing a transformation, releasing the fullness of life and the passion God designed them to live—a companion Participant's Guide is also available! The Fathered by God Small Group Video Series includes:

- 1 DVD of 8 sessions
- 1 CD-ROM with promotional and church campaign resources
- Leader's Guide
- Spanish track included